# MARY'S WAY

## Cultivating a Peaceful Heart in Trying Times

*From Anne*

*Peace be with you,*

*Peggy Tabor Millin*

## PEGGY TABOR MILLIN

**STORY WATER PRESS**

**STORY WATER PRESS**
**Asheville, North Carolina**

Story Water Press is pleased to publish this third printing of *Mary's Way*.

Celestial Arts, Berkeley, CA, first published *Mary's Way* in 1990 and again in 1995. Those printings contain photographs that have been omitted here. They can be viewed at www.clarityworksonline.com.

June 24, 2011 marked the thirtieth anniversary of the beginning of the apparitions.

Material quoted from *The Caritas Newsletter*, November / December 1989 issue and March / April 1990 issue reprinted by permission of *The Caritas Newsletter*, 100 Our Lady Queen of Peace Dr., Sterett, AL 36147.

Quotation from *Words from Heaven*, a book of Our Lady's messages from Medjugorje, reprinted by permission of St. James Publishing, PO Box 380244, Birmingham, AL 35238-0244.

Quotation from Swami Muktananda reprinted from *Reflections of the Self*, by Swami Muktananda (South Fallsburg, NY: SYDA Foundation, 1980), reprinted by permission of SYDA Foundation.

ISBN 978-0-9823711-5-2

Cover and Book Design by Ginger Graziano Design Group  www.gingergraziano.com

Author's photograph by Max Poppers, Silver Spirits Photography
www.silverspiritsphotography.com

STORY WATER PRESS
PO Box 9803
Asheville, North Carolina 28815

*Blessed are the peacemakers:*
*for they shall be called*
*the children of God.*
~ MATTHEW 5:9

# CONTENTS

*Oh Great Spirit*
*Light a candle in my heart*
*that I may see the rubbish*
*in Thy dwelling place*
*and sweep it clean.*

~ American Indian prayer

# ACKNOWLEDGMENTS

I make grateful acknowledgments to: LOUIS MILLIN, my husband and my partner on the path of life. Walking with him is my great joy. ERIC, GRANT, and KAREN, my children, who have been my teachers. I truly honor the path each has chosen. EARL DAVIS and CAROLYN WALLACE, my dear friends, who have believed in me and have honored me with their love, LOUIS ALEXANDER who helped me believe I could write and FATHER FRANK GARDNER whose openness has been a blessing and whose comments on the manuscript were invaluable. The INSTITUTE FOR THE ADVANCEMENT OF SERVICE, Alexandria, VA, which has been my spiritual home and school. NEIL VAHLE, former editor of *New Realities* magazine, who published my article, "The Message of Medjugorje." JOY O'ROURKE, consulting editor of *New Realities* magazine, who did a masterful job of editing the article. JO ANN DECK of Celestial Arts Publishers, who saw the article and invited me to write this book. She has encouraged and helped me greatly along the way.

And to my friends on the QUALLA BOUNDARY, especially those at and connected with the CHEROKEE CENTRAL SCHOOLS, *Nigada otsadatseli*, "All my relations." You have truly provided me with endless opportunities to learn to give and receive love.


*To my friend SUSAN S. TROUT*
*who gave me the trip to Medjugorje and*
*who has strewn my spiritual path with roses.*

# INTRODUCTION
# TO THE FIRST EDITION 1991

THIS IS A BOOK FOR ORDINARY PEOPLE. It is not about supernatural events, rather it is about the most natural of events—the experience of Love in its most sublime form. Whatever events lead one to this experience, they will always be imbued with a special quality. For after all, when one has a holy experience, one then ascribes holiness to the events surrounding it.

This particular event is the appearance since 1981 of the Virgin Mary to six Yugoslavian young people in the small village of Medjugorje. This event is not Catholic in the sense of that particular denomination. It is catholic in the sense that the word means "universal." Mary has indicated to the children in Medjugorje that all people are the children of God regardless of their chosen religions. It is man who has created the divisions in the world; in God there is no separation. So it is true that the event is not Christian in the strict sense, although it is about Christ Consciousness. This event is not about religion; it is about spiritual growth and empowerment. This is an event that even if you deny its possibility, you are asked to stay open to its message.

I went to Medjugorje in March 1989 and subsequently wrote "Medjugorje: One Pilgrim's Perspective," an article that appeared in the March-April 1990 edition of *New Realities* magazine and which appears here as the first chapter. My experience in Medjugorje changed my life.

A physical pilgrimage is a ritual act, an outer manifestation of our search for an inner destination. A pilgrimage is a journey to our innermost being. A specific physical site attracts us by symbolizing something beyond ourselves that we deeply desire to experience. A pilgrimage, then, is an act of surrender in which we offer ourselves to the Divine Source.

Simply by the sincere willingness to embark upon a pilgrimage, we are transformed. Through willingness, we have opened our hearts. How close we come to this inner destination in our daily lives is related to our degree of willingness and surrender.

This book is born of my personal study and my spiritual growth before, at, and after Medjugorje. It is not meant to be a pervasive or persuasive study of Mary or the events and messages of Medjugorje. It is in a very real sense my search for the ethereal Mary of whose presence I am now ever aware. Mary asks us to transcend our individual differences, not to eradicate them. So in this book I attempt to share what I have integrated within myself as bridges among traditional Christianity, metaphysics, and mysticism. This integration is on the level of the heart, not the mind. You are asked to approach it with your heart open.

The message is necessarily delivered in Christian terminology and reflects Catholic form. For many this will make it difficult to hear. Reflect on this: spiritual truth is beyond words and form; for this truth there are no words. Religion is the form: spiritual truth has no form. It simply IS. As humans, we seek to understand that which is beyond understanding. The best we can do at times is simply to ask the Divine Source to clear our minds and to allow whatever truth is present to touch us.*

When we meet God for however brief a moment and however experienced, we separate out that event, seeing it as the exception. It is in fact possible for it to be the rule. We are not introduced to God in a moment of revelation or in a dream or on a pilgrimage so that we can isolate and frame that moment in our memory. We are given that moment as our heritage and our right so that we can see that our whole life can BE that moment and that we can live with and in that incredible Love every moment.

We all have access to this Love. It is after all the one thing that all people everywhere throughout time have yearned for—to be loved un-

---

* One of the religious traditions most disturbing to women is the continued use of the masculine as the universal marker of person and of the Divine. I made every attempt to circumvent this when I had a choice; however, because the subject is based on Christian form, the use of the masculine has been unavoidable.

conditionally with no limitations. This deep desire to be loved is perhaps what truly makes us human. We seek it in relationships with each other, in money, food, and addictions and never find it. There could be a universal riddle or koan: What does every person seek, many never find, and yet all already have? The answer is Divine Unconditional Love. If what makes us human is our desire for Love, then what makes us recognize our divinity is our experience of Love fulfilled.

This is a book about ordinary people and a particular event that has touched millions of lives, making it possible for them to claim what has always been theirs—Divine Love.

This book is one way in which I can share myself. I have learned that as long as I give of my peace, my insight, and my love, I will keep them and will continue to grow in them. It is very important to me that you, the reader, understand that everything I have done or experienced or learned is open to you also. We are all students and teachers at the same time and for one another. The spiritual path is not a classroom in which grades are given and rankings are made. It is an open classroom in which we tutor one another, share our experiences, and learn at our own rate in our own style. The goal of our learning is to reconnect with God from whom we have separated ourselves.

Whatever ways you have found bring you closer to God, practice them.

However you can become more loving, more compassionate, more forgiving, more accepting of your own limitations and those of your neighbor, do that.

The only way in which we can save our planet, save our children, and find joy in our lives today is through forgetting differences and recognizing our oneness. In other words—in finding God within ourselves and one another.

As you look within your self to discover your own connection with the Divine, remember to be compassionate with yourself, to heal the wounds that have kept you feeling separate from your neighbor and from God, and to forgive your self. These things are necessary to be at peace within; then you will have an enormous capacity to share your self with others.

Mary appears in Medjugorje as the Universal Mother who nurtures, protects, and guides. She chose six children simply for their ordinariness. By doing so, she speaks to us all.

Our job is to listen and to do what she asks without fear.

This is Mary's Way.

*You will discover God in everything,*
*even in the smallest flower.*
*You will discover a great joy.*
*You will discover God!*
~ April 25, 1989

# PREFACE
# TO THE SECOND PRINTING 1995

SINCE THE INITIAL PUBLICATION OF *MARY'S WAY* IN 1991, tragic changes have occurred in the physical world of Medjugorje, Bosnia-Hercegovina, and the one-time nation of Yugoslavia. The seeds of discord among ethnic and religious groups in the Balkan states are as ancient as those groups themselves. Yugoslavia came into existence as a single political entity only following World War I. Geographically as well as religiously, politically, and culturally, it has been, and still is, the crossroads and collision point of eastern and western civilizations.

In the 1930s, the monarchist Serbs fought the nationalistic Croats, the latter of which were supported by Mussolini and the Italian Fascist party. The Croats held a bloody reign of power for many years (with help from Germany once Italy pulled out of World War II) until the Allied forces ordered the surrender of arms to a non-partisan group of both Serbs and Croats under the leadership of Croat Josip Tito. Tito was fairly successful in neutralizing the situation by scattering the Serbian population among the republics. However, with his death in 1980, the government was left to founder for ten years until it eventually collapsed in January of 1990 in a disarray of economic, social, and political upheaval.

Complex and opposing agendas continue to challenge its unification—Croatian nationalism stands at odds with Serbian demands for equal political power, while discord between Roman Catholic (largely Croat) and Eastern Orthodox (largely Serb) churches grows. Meanwhile, a growing Muslim population also crosses ethnic lines.

In the 1991 Bosnian vote for independence, the Muslims and Croats favored independence whereas the Serbs boycotted the vote, wishing to stay with Serbia and Montenegro as part of Yugoslavia. When Bosnia-Hercegovina was recognized as a separate nation, the Serbs proclaimed a Serbian Bosnian state, a disagreement that led to a civil war now in its fourth year. Medjugorje, the village where the sightings have occurred, is located in Bosnia-Hercegovina and is hence directly vulnerable to the pillage and destruction. However, while numerous nearby towns have been completely destroyed, Medjugorje has remained largely intact. It is not difficult to believe that this village has been under the special protection of Our Lady. While other religious symbols have been prime targets, St. James church stands untouched. Large crowds continue to gather for holiday celebrations without disturbance and pilgrims still flock to the site. As an island of relative safety, Medjugorje has been used both as the United Nations Headquarters and as a hospice for refugees, particularly orphaned children. It is generally accepted, apparently even by the Serbs, that something greater than the Croatian artillery protects this tiny town, its church, and those who live and worship there.

As tragic as these circumstances may be, it is well beyond the scope of this book to explain the whole history of this region's turmoil. The references made to the former nation of Yugoslavia remain because they refer to the time and the place the visions occurred (long prior to the outbreak of war) and therefore most appropriately convey my experience.

~PTM. Asheville, North Carolina, 1995

# INTRODUCTION
# TO THE SECOND EDITION 2011

THIRTY YEARS AGO ON JUNE 24, 1981, six young people near the village of Medjugorje, Bosnia-Hercegovina (formerly part of Yugoslavia), saw an apparition of Mary, mother of Jesus, who later identified herself as Queen of Peace. Mary still appears on a daily basis to three of the visionaries wherever they are, including in the United States. The other three visionaries no longer see her daily; she appears to them annually on specific dates.

How I, a non-Catholic, came to make a pilgrimage to Medjugorje and to write, publish, and republish *Mary's Way* felt orchestrated by a divine hand. Now, twenty years after that trip, I hear a gentle voice saying, "It's time," and I know what is wanted.

This time of global transition as humanity awakens to the emergence of the power of the feminine is the time for which *Mary's Way* was intended. The original publication allowed me to put the story on paper while fresh and inspired; it planted seeds of the message in the minds and hearts of others. As happened, the Bosnian War broke out shortly before publication by Celestial Arts and the demand for pilgrimages and the book diminished. After one reprinting, it went out of print. Now free to align the book with my own heart, I have given it a subtitle that reflects its original purpose: *Cultivating a Peaceful Heart in Trying Times*.

Mary comes as a guide to recognizing and accepting the kingdom of heaven abiding already within us. She synthesizes feminine/masculine energies: creativity/action, body/mind, intuition/thinking. She wants us to ground ourselves firmly in our inner kingdom—which can also be thought of as strengthening the connection between our personal soul and the Transpersonal Soul. By cultivating a peaceful heart, we stand steadfast as the world goes through the physical changes needed to bring about a change of consciousness. Steadfast and peaceful hearts embody courage— the will to act from selfless love—and thus we serve without collapsing into fear.

On foggy nights on the Blue Ridge Parkway, the car's headlamps disappear into the mist some fifty feet ahead. The dense forest closes in on both sides and joins with the fog to shield the road from the ambient light of nearby towns. Even though I am familiar with the Parkway's hilly twists, the absence of landmarks disorients me. I am alone and isolated, anxious lest I miss the exit that leads me home.

If I could see beyond the pavement ahead, I would sink into the false security of believing my trip to be predictable, that my knowledge of driving in this familiar area insures safe travel, and that in a crisis my cell phone can summon help. Blinded by the thick night, however, I am reminded that security is even more of an illusion than is dependable cell service in the mountains. My safety lies in allowing the headlights to guide me while I watch for signs.

This practice of moment-to-moment vigilance is Mary's way to a peaceful heart.

Years ago I heard a story about the Dalai Lama that took place while he was teaching in the United States. After days of teaching in which he emphasized the need for continual practice through meditation and daily action, he asked for questions. The first questioner asked how quickly the United States would achieve enlightenment. Apparently dismayed that the questioner had missed the message of the week's teachings, the Dalai Lama removed his glasses and wept with his face in his hands. Silence settled over the audience as they witnessed his grief. Finally he replaced his glasses and faced them. His answer was spoken with vehemence. "Not fast. Not easy. Not cheap."

The spiritual journey has no "get rich quick" scheme. All great spiritual teachers insist that we must do the work, stay the course, and practice, practice, practice. In this way, we become the path we travel.

**Not fast.** The spiritual journey is inward. An inward journey does not follow the outer world's concept of time, but reveals itself step by step. Mary emphasizes the continual prayer through which we practice gratitude, relationship, forgiveness, and listening for and following inner guidance. We overcome obstacles by seeing them as lessons. Through practice our whole life becomes a prayer. Through life as prayer we serve.

**Not easy.** To make the spiritual journey requires dedication, commitment, and discipline. Unless we travel with this wholehearted intention we may be absorbed by the darkness and miss the signs leading home. Complacency and pride present great dangers that lead us to take detours and even to drive off cliffs.

**Not cheap.** The spiritual journey has no monetary value, yet is the pearl of great price of which Jesus spoke. In *Holy the Firm*, author Annie Dillard writes:

> The secret of seeing is, then, the pearl of great price. If I thought he could teach me to find it and keep it forever I would stagger barefoot across a hundred deserts after any lunatic at all. But although the pearl may be found, it may not be sought. The literature of illumination reveals this above all: although it comes to those who wait for it, it is always, even to the most practiced and adept, a gift and a total surprise.

The spiritual journey has no goal, nothing tangible to grasp, not even a permanent state of being. As I understand it, enlightenment comes in flashes of insight that last as long as they last. Such flashes arise from shifting our focus from the material world to the inner life of the soul. Our outer life then becomes a reflection of our inner reality: increasingly the heart rests in peace and selfless service replaces striving. This shift in focus rearranges our priorities; we give up what no longer serves this higher purpose and are occasionally surprised by glimpses of the resplendent pearl of great price.

On this journey, the message of *Mary's Way* provides a beam of light shining on the path. Mary speaks straight to our hearts. Hers is one voice of many telling us to practice prayer as communion with God and to seek forgiveness from those we have wronged and to extend it to those we believe have wronged us. She has no agenda but to offer us a path to walk upon. She wants us to change our minds, to decide for Love so we can deepen our consciousness and open our hearts to our interconnection with one another and with God. Moment to moment, we follow the light on the path, look for signs, and cultivate a peaceful heart.

Other than corrections, minor changes, and the 2011 Information Update following Chapter 1, this edition of *Mary's Way* is the version reprinted in 1995. Since that time, I have become a student of Soto Zen Buddhism and my understanding has changed in this and many other aspects as I have followed Mary's way. In subsequent books, I will write the synchronistic story of how the book was initially born and of how I now view this life-changing event. The photographs originally contained in the book can be viewed on my website, clarityworksonline.com.

For more information about Medjugorje, the messages, and the visionaries, please go to medjugorje.com. Be aware that after the first decade of the apparitions, the information about the visionaries and the messages themselves shifted in tone, becoming more conservative, rigid, and dogmatic. Around this time I discovered I had been named a heretic by a Catholic magazine. Even so, many priests, monks, nuns, and faithful Catholics along with Buddhists and Protestants continue to embrace the message of *Mary's Way*, keeping it on their nightstands for inspiration. I believe that the inclusive and loving quality in her early messages reflects Mary's true intent.

And so once again, I willingly take my experience and send it out into the world.

~PTM. Asheville, North Carolina, 2011

## CHAPTER ONE

# MEDJUGORJE:
# ONE PILGRIM'S PERSPECTIVE

*God is Father; but above all, God is Mother.*
~ POPE JOHN PAUL II

SINCE JUNE 24, 1981, MEDJUGORJE, a small village located in a harsh, mountainous area of the former Yugoslavian republic of Bosnia-Hercegovina, has lent its name to the world as the destination of thousands of pilgrims. On that date, six young people from the neighboring town of Bijakovići say that they witnessed the appearance of the Blessed Mother, the Virgin Mary. The apparitions have continued to date, making them the longest-running series of Marian visitations in history.

Medjugorje's chronology of events began on that June day when sixteen-year-old Mirjana Dragicević walked with her friend Ivanka Ivanković, fifteen, near a hilltop called Podbrodo. Ivanka first noticed a luminous silhouette suspended above the ground on a cloud, and exclaimed, "Mirjana, look there is Our Lady, the Blessed Mother."

Because the Yugoslav authorities have confiscated the original tape-recorded chronology of these early events, there is some confusion remains as to the young people originally involved. But it is known that it was Mirjana and Ivanka and four of their friends, Ivan Dragicević, sixteen, Vicka Ivanković, seventeen, Marija Pavlović, sixteen, and Jakov Čolov, ten, who were to continue to witness the apparitions. These six returned to the hill the second day and were beckoned up the mountain by the apparition.

While watched by two adults, the youths were literally swooped up the hill in five minutes, a walk which usually takes at least twenty minutes.

By the third day, as the news of the apparition spread, several thousand people encircled the young visionaries at the base of the mountain. This time the apparition was preceded by a brilliant light observed by all present; only the six young people, however, could see the actual apparition. The Holy Mother told the children, "I have come because there are many believers here. I want to be with you to convert and reconcile everyone." She closed her visit as she would all subsequent visits, "Go in the peace of God."[1]

My friend Susan Trout, director of the Institute for the Advancement of Service in Alexandria, Virginia, returned from the site in August 1988 and shared her experiences with me. Intrigued by the inner changes she and others reported to have undergone during their pilgrimages there, I became determined to go to Medjugorje myself. Fortuitously, Susan invited me to act as chronicler of a March 1989 pilgrimage sponsored by the Institute.

Our group of twenty-nine was distinguished by its predominantly non-Catholic background. We came to this pilgrimage instead as students of metaphysics, willing to step through whatever barriers had caused most of us to leave mainstream Christianity or Judaism in order to immerse ourselves during our pilgrimages in the words, rituals, and symbols of the traditions we had previously rejected. I do not believe that any of us realized then that simply by going to Medjugorje we would each begin or continue our individual processes of forgiveness toward all the differences we each had previously perceived between "our" beliefs and "theirs."

Raised as a Methodist and trained in neuropsychology, I have for many years been a seeker on the spiritual path, pursuing metaphysics, various personal growth approaches, *A Course in Miracles*, and Siddha Yoga. Although committed to spiritual study and practice, I am not a devotee or a follower of any particular group. My fascination with others' inner experiences awakened both curiosity and spiritual yearning for some knowingness that I did not seem to have, some connection to God that I had not yet been able to feel. I had had a profound personal spiritual awakening the previous summer following an intensive personal growth workshop, but I could not seem to hold onto the experience. I could not or did not make it real in my life. I welcomed the pilgrimage to Medjugorje as an opportunity to seek the spiritual knowingness and connection that had been eluding me.

The Yugoslav authorities grew increasingly concerned about the gathering crowds at Medjugorje and the ensuing publicity. The lessons of history had taught them that even the hint of a strong religious movement was cause for concern about a possible nationalistic rebellion. As a result, four days after the first apparition, the visionaries were summoned to police headquarters in Čitluk, where they were seen by doctors, assessed by them as psychologically healthy and released. Later that day, during the now-daily 30- to 45-minute apparition, the figure formally identified herself to them as "the Blessed Virgin Mary." Even Ivan, who had not accompanied the others on this day, received a visit from the Blessed Mother while he was alone, away from the mountain.

By June 28, 1981, a crowd of 15,000 had gathered at the base of Mt. Podbrodo. During this visit, the visionaries asked prepared questions, several of which dealt with why everyone could not see her and what she wanted of all the people gathered. Her response was that it was important that people believe without seeing.

That following day, the visionaries were again summoned to police headquarters in Čitluk for questioning and examination, and were again pronounced to be mentally stable. During the following visitation, they requested that the Blessed Mother give them some sign of authenticity to relieve the pressure from the village adults and from the authorities. They specifically requested the healing of a small, mute, physically disabled boy named Daniel. According to a written account of an interview with the boy's parents by Abbé René Laurentin, a renowned French Mariologist who has written extensively on Medjugorje, the boy was healed.

In preparation for our inner pilgrimage to Medjugorje, it was suggested to those in our group that we meditate on specific questions or reasons we had for going. The two requests that emerged for me were (1) to be given a more open heart in order to be more loving and (2) to be taught how to pray. Shortly before leaving, a string of events in my life led me to add a third request: to learn the meaning of surrender. My first two requests were answered in Medjugorje; the response to my third came after my return home.

As part of my preparation, I attempted to open my mind and heart to anything that might occur there. When I arrived in Medjugorje, however, I found myself openly denying that I could personally experience anything meaningful during my pilgrimage. I had read that other pilgrims had experienced great peace, seen the sun dance, heard voices, and seen visions. I was very vocal about the unlikelihood that I would have such experiences myself. In my journal I wrote, "A part of me says that I will be the only person here not to have some profound experience. Another part says, 'So what?'" At that point, I gave up my expectations for what might happen and began to accept just being there.

In the journal in which I kept daily entries of what happened both outside and within myself during the trip, I observed on March 19, 1989 (Palm Sunday and the commencement of our pilgrimage):

"The sounds of the Croatian Mass come over the loudspeakers, the local people on benches outside and swelling from the open doorways give their responses, and during the consecration of the Eucharist, they move forward to kiss the wall of the church. The sound is mesmerizing and I begin to understand the meaning of ritual. It is like a mantra that takes one immediately to that Inner Room.

"Later, I walk up Podbrodo, the Hill of the Apparitions, where Mary is said to have first appeared to the two girls while they were out gathering the sheep. The climb is steep and incredibly rocky. Crosses, mostly placed by pilgrims, stud the pathway; one marks the place of the first apparition. The main one at the crest of the hill is set in a pile of rocks on which pilgrims have left candles and petitions. The atmosphere is quiet and peaceful, that of a holy place, a sanctuary above the valley. Groups come and go, rosaries are said in different languages; some people sit alone in meditation.

"As I walk down the hill to reach St. James in time for the daily Rosary, during which the apparition is said to occur, I notice a certain unwillingness among pilgrims to meet one another's eyes. Strange, in this place whose message is a call to inner peace through extending love and peace to others, that people remain so separate. I find a place to stand in the already crowded church and pull out my newly purchased rosary beads. The prayers begin. As they are said in Croatian and I am unfamiliar with the sequence, I am lost. The words of one of the group leaders come back to me, 'Mary is not a person; Mary is a heart space. If you cannot say the Rosary, just say whatever is in your heart.' My prayer becomes, 'Mother-Father-God, I come to you in peace and surrender. Let me see Thy Light that it may fill my heart, that I may share it with others.'

"The priest asks for silence and in several languages explains that it is time for the apparition to occur in the choir loft. I feel the energy shift during this time, something tangible yet indescribable. I turn to leave after the Rosary and encounter the eyes of an Austrian woman standing several rows back. Her blonde wig and unnatural suntanned look suggest radiation treatment for cancer. Our eyes lock and my arms open. She steps into them and we embrace silently for a long time, and then we exchange a deep look of love. Maybe this is the blessing of Medjugorje."

During the first days of the apparitions, the village priest was Father Jozo Zovko. He had been advising and counseling the visionaries, but he had not taken a strong supportive role until exactly one week after the initial vision when the police decided to take the six youths into custody and pursued them to the mountain. The young people ran back to the village and to the church. Father Jozo was praying when he heard a voice say, "Come out and protect the children." He ran out just as the visionaries arrived and hid them in the church while the police searched in another direction.

Interference by the police continued. They made it illegal for the public to convene at Mt. Podbrodo. The apparitions continued but now in homes and on the hills around the village.

In October 1981, Father Jozo was tried and convicted by the government of disobedience and encouraging unrest in the community. He was sentenced to three-and-a-half years in prison; later this was reduced to eighteen months. Father Jozo is now the priest for a neighboring parish. Until recently, he was not allowed to return to Medjugorje.

During our stay, we were able to hear Vicka and Ivan speak, as well as meet with Father Slavko Barbarić, current mentor to the visionaries, and Father Petar Ljubičić, the priest selected to communicate to the world the secrets revealed by the Virgin to the children. We also traveled to a nearby parish to meet with Father Jozo Zovko, their early supporter.

The visionaries themselves struck me as very ordinary people; in fact, when they asked the Blessed Mother why she chose them, she replied that it was because of their "ordinariness"—she needed them exactly as they were.

Throughout the years of the apparitions, although the visionaries have been tested by psychiatrists and medical doctors as well as questioned, threatened, held by the police, and denounced by their own bishop, they have continued to give their accounts of the visions with few discrepancies. Certainly, their lives have not been made easier by these experiences. Nevertheless, since 1981, they have continued to see the apparitions, some daily, some annually, whether at home in Medjugorje or at one of the universities several are now attending. Marija, Mirjana, and Ivan have visited the United States and received visitations from Mary while here.

The long-standing animosity and political friction between the Franciscan Brothers and the Yugoslav Roman Catholic church has been at the heart of most of the controversy over the apparitions at Medjugorje. The first commission appointed by the church to determine the legitimacy of the apparitions was disbanded when it failed to reach a verdict by the end of 1983.

A second commission was formed and chaired by Pavao Žanić, the Bishop of the diocese of Mostar of which St. James parish in Medjugorje is a part. Although initially supportive of the apparitions, Žanić inexplicably became an avowed critic of the happenings in Medjugorje and in 1984 sent an opposition report to all the bishops around the world and to the press, giving the impression that Rome itself had spoken out against pilgrimages to Medjugorje. Not surprisingly, on May 2, 1986, the second commission voted against the legitimacy of the apparitions; the bishop informed the local Franciscans that by the end of June, Medjugorje could no longer be a destination of Catholic pilgrims.

According to Father Slavko Barbarić, Rome's reaction to the second commission's report was unprecedented in history. Instead of supporting the commission's view and ordering a stop to the apparitions, Rome ordered Bishop Žanić to cease hostilities and established a third, unbiased commission that is still studying the question of the legitimacy of the apparitions.

During 1982, the Blessed Mother told the visionaries that she would reveal ten secrets to each individually. The secrets concern the private lives of the visionaries, the life of the villagers, and the world at large. Only one secret has been revealed: the Blessed Mother's promise to leave a sign on Mt. Podbrodo at the end of the apparitions to prove their validity to the world. Before this visible sign, there will be three warnings on Earth to allow people to return to God. *See 2011 Information Update at end of this chapter.*

*In your life you have all experienced
light and darkness.
God grants to every person recognition
of good and evil. I am calling
you to the light which you should
carry to all the people who are in
darkness. People who are in darkness
daily come into your homes.
Dear children, give them the light!*
~ March 14, 1985

The ninth and tenth secrets describe chastisement for the world; although inevitable and serious, the chastisement can be mitigated through prayer and fasting. The evil that threatened the world as revealed in the seventh secret has already been mitigated through prayer. The Blessed Mother says, "You have forgotten that with prayer and fasting you can ward off wars and suspend natural laws."

Mirjana claims to have been given a paper inscribed with all ten secrets. To a group of Italian tourists she described this as "of an indescribable material. It seems like paper but it isn't.... You can touch it but not see the writing on it.... When the right moment comes, I am to give it to a specially chosen priest, who will then be given the grace to read only the first secret from it."[2] In the same year, two other young people, Jelena Vasilij and her friend Marijana Vasilij (not related), began receiving messages from the Blessed Mother by inner locution (hearing rather than seeing Her).

By the summer of 1984, the length of the apparitions had been reduced to a minute or less. In response to the Madonna's suggestion of a three-day feast honoring her 2,000th birthday, 35,000 people gathered in Medjugorje.

My journal entry of March 20, 1989 recounts an experience I had while sitting outside in the churchyard listening to Father Petar and Father Slavko: "'Look at the sun!' someone says. I look and see a grey disc to the side of the sun. I can see the round shape of the sun, too, not obscured by its brightness. The disc moves across the sun and I can look without pain or blindness. The sun pulsates and swirls. A huge magenta circle appears around the sun; the color changes to green, then blue with a green edge.

"I look away in doubt. No spots appear before my eyes; there is no effect from having looked at the sun for several minutes. I look back and see that there is also a golden cloud that moves into the sun with the disc. All who look see it and all who see it are amazed. Yet no one falls to the ground, cries out in fear, or expresses any unusual reaction. Instead we cease watching, although the phenomenon continues, and proceed to decide where to have lunch. I muse over the meaning of this."

Dr. Denis Janz[3] suggests that it is the desire for "religious certitude," the desire to have some concrete proof that one's faith is justified, that sends many on the pilgrimage. Yet, when given such concrete proof in the church-yard, none of us reacted as though our faith had suddenly proven justified. Nor was it received as a life changing "sign" for those of us assembled.

Many come to Medjugorje for physical cures and many believe that cures have actually taken place. Official church verification and acceptance of such claims—as has long been the case at Lourdes—will take many years. I believe that the miracles of Medjugorje, and miracles in general, do not occur in a church choir loft with apparitions or in seeing the sun spin or in physical healing. The true miracle occurs *within* the pilgrim, even one who never leaves home.

BBC journalist Mary Craig quotes a September, 1986 BBC interview with Father Jozo Zovko in her book *Spark from Heaven*.[4] In the interview, the priest tells of two invalided Italian women.

> The elder of the two women was healed. The younger, Manuela, remained in her wheelchair. The one who was healed returned home, delighted at being able to walk again; Manuela stayed be-hind to give thanks and praise to God. They had both come with the desire to be healed, and they were both healed. But heal-ing is not only physical, it is something that takes place in the heart. Manuela was healed in her heart. Full of joy, she praised God for having come to her, for shedding light on the cross she carried, for showing her its value and meaning. She understood that from her wheelchair she could bring people spiritual solace, telling them about the love of God, about goodness, about the wisdom that patience can bring. Manuela took a far greater joy home in her heart than the woman who went home able to walk. The Church was grateful for both blessings. Deeply grateful.

The Blessed Mother says that we do not have to journey to Medjugorje to have this experience of inner peace; we can obtain it at home. What she has suggested and advised the visionaries (she never demands) is a consistent regimen of prayer and fasting.

"Pray" and "prayer"—meaning "communion with God"—are the most common words in the Blessed Mother's messages. The form of the prayer—meditation, verbal petitions, or use of scriptures—does not matter; the intent and sincerity of the prayer is what is important.

She stresses that the goal is to pray without ceasing, to develop a consciousness in which one's thoughts are always on God. Prayer is a symbol of a commitment to the spiritual life. Mary emphasizes the joy of prayer and says that, through prayer, one will receive guidance from the Inner Voice. Although the Blessed Mother's exhortations are always to the "children," it is apparent that she considers all of us to be her children. The messages are for everyone, not just for the Medjugorje visionaries.

The Blessed Mother, in her messages to the visionaries, also admonishes the faithful to fast—to abstain from things that take us away from peace. She has instructed that, when we are together, we "not talk together about anything and everything, but of things concerning faith, prayer, and peace." This is fasting in its broadest sense.

Pope John Paul II pronounced 1987 the Marian Year. Although the Pope has been informed of the events at Medjugorje, the Catholic Church has not announced the validity of the apparitions. *(See Information Update at end of this chapter)* It is significant that during the Marian Year, Father Stefano Gobbi, founder of the National Directors of the Marian Movement of Priests, reported a direct message for the priests from the Blessed Mother during the group's annual retreat.

As I note in my journal entry of March 22, 1989, because of the joy I am finding in prayer, many thoughts are beginning to emerge as to why I am here and what this all means to me on my spiritual journey. Among them are:

❖ Mary is the feminine energy that can save the world; we have had enough of the aggressive, manipulative side. It is time for nurturance and intuition; a time to embrace and support our Earth and one another. If Mary's messages are apocalyptic, it is because we have created the apocalypse.

❖ A pilgrimage allows time and space for dedication, an opportunity to confront some major issues that occur in daily life and to move through them in peace. Despite the frustration of dealing with the cacophony of languages and customs encountered here, the shoving crowds and sometimes trying hygienic conditions, one can—as I learned at Medjugorje— easily confront all of these things from a place of deep peace.

❖ A pilgrimage to Medjugorje allows one to deal with releasing expectations—both in terms of what will happen here, as well as an expectation of what a spiritual experience is. It appears from talking to the other pilgrims that each gets what is needed for that individual at the appropriate moment.

❖ Truth transcends. Regardless of whether we are Baptists, Catholics, Muslims, Jewish, followers of Eastern religious traditions, or non-believers, we are all guilty of making judgments and separations on the basis of our differences in beliefs. I sit in this simple church and suddenly realize how lost in *form* I have become. For years, I have judged the statues and rosaries and crucifixes as being "unenlightened." In a flash, I realize that they are really no different from crystals and mandalas and the Sanskrit Om. They are all merely symbols of the One Source, reminders to keep us on the path or tools to use in our practice of Oneness. When I react negatively to someone else's symbol or someone else's word for God, I know I have an attachment to give up. If the form does not matter to God, why need it matter to me?

All these things came to me at Medjugorje. Mary says to follow the greatest commandment, "To love God with all your heart and all your soul and all your might," using whatever form is the most comfortable. She also tells us that we must love our neighbors as ourselves, which means without judgment or feelings of separation.

The Yugoslav government quickly recognized the isolated mountain village of Medjugorje as a commercial mecca. Many of the townspeople have left their vineyards and sheep- and goat-herding occupations in order to serve the thousands who come daily from around the world to stay in their homes and eat at their tables. The tourist industry at the site grows daily.

Entering St. James Church on my last day at Medjugorje, as I write in my journal entry of March 23, 1989:

"I am aware of a soft sadness at leaving the sense of peace that has slowly descended within me during the week. The church is virtually empty; it is Maundy Thursday, and there are no masses. It is the first time I have entered without pushing through throngs of local Croatians and pilgrims murmuring prayers in different tongues.

"The simplicity of the church strikes me anew. Rows of pews, polished now by the devotion of the hundreds of thousands who have come in the past eight years, stand empty and expectant. The altar is unadorned except for a beautifully embroidered cloth; a large plain wooden cross stands in the back to one side, a copy of the stone one on Cross Hill. High above the nave, contemporary stained glass windows depict Mary in the life of Jesus and the story of the apparitions.

"Incense wafts past; some nuns scurry around the altar making Easter preparations. The peace descends again as I make my way to the Mary altar on the right side of the church. I have been near it once and did not find the Mary statue especially appealing. Mary, smaller than life-size, stands in gilt-edged white shawl and blue robe with hands held in prayer. I name her 'The Blue Madonna.'

"Suddenly it is as though some great force within pushes up and out through my heart; my heart feels as though it physically opens and any sorrow that I had hidden away before is forced into light. I am acutely aware of the Oneness of all being and the incredible healing and all-encompassing Power of the universe.

"Physically, I am sure I stop breathing, tears run down my cheeks. 'I cannot leave this!' I think. 'I can't go.' Caught in that bliss, I know what until then I had only 'known', and there is no place I want to be other than right here in whatever this is. The feeling of all-encompassing love is so great that I know this is what I have searched for my whole life. Gently, I feel myself being pushed away and I hear a voice within saying, 'Take this and go out into the world.'"

One of Mary's transmissions to the visionaries is:

"You know that I wish to guide you on the way of holiness, but I do not want to force you. I do not want you to be holy by force. I wish every one of you to help yourselves and me by your little sacrifices so that I can guide you to be more holy day by day. Therefore, dear children, I do not want to force you to live the messages; but rather this long time I am with you shows that I love you immeasurably and that I wish every single one of you to be holy."

When I returned home, I could scarcely function in the daily world because I was in such a state of bliss! I found that people for whom I had prayed in Medjugorje had had shifts in their lives while I was gone. I began receiving messages for people while I was in prayer—I, who had never before "heard" or "seen" things, found myself receiving answers for other people.

In time, I understood that the gift of this for me was not in the ability to receive the messages but in surrendering my own will. (Confronting a professional acquaintance with a message that came through prayer is risky and difficult.) I also discovered how much easier it is to ignore what one is hearing, and, on one occasion, I argued with my Inner Voice for two hours because I did not want to do what I was being asked. Each step is small, but of increasing difficulty. Each time now that I think that I cannot possibly comply, I am assured that it is absolutely safe. These lessons continue and, so far, none of my fears has been realized; the journey to surrender—a goal I set up to achieve during my pilgrimage—has thus far been safe.

I had long understood that surrender has nothing to do with "giving up"; however, only upon my return from Medjugorje did I learn that surrender really means totally loving myself, with all my human frailties and shortcomings. In Medjugorje, I experienced the love of God; now I find that surrender involves accepting this love for myself.

The most profound transformation in my post-Medjugorje life concerns my relationship with my husband. I had previously been prone to periodic blaming attacks, for which I would feel guilty and from which he would withdraw. Upon my return I saw him in a new way—as one who loved me in a way that I often rejected.

Yes, I still am prone to respond to my husband and children in my "old way." But now, although the words—by habit—may be the same, the emotional content is absent in my attacking responses. I've come to realize that I no longer need these in my life. As a result, a lot of my old "acts" have dropped away. Further, I find myself now more committed than ever to searching inside for the underlying causes of my actions. Once found, I can let them go more easily.

My life has become much more purposeful, positive, and full of abundance since my pilgrimage. And, despite the temptation to revert to old patterns, I find I can focus my attention better, that I can be present for people in need in a supportive way without feeling incompetent to answer their needs. I also find more joy in my life.

Of course, I did not have to go to Medjugorje for this transformation. Neither did I have to be a certain kind of person or have a certain belief system. God is no respecter of persons or places and, I believe, is not nearly so tied up in points of view as we are!

Father Jozo, quoted in Craig's *Spark from Heaven*,[5] reminds us that the gift of God's Spirit is always the same regardless of the medium through which it is transmitted; that whatever messages are being received, they are merely "different dimensions of the source of life." It is this "source of life" that we all seek, no matter who we are. I believe that all it takes to receive the gift is sincere willingness.

As I noted in an earlier journal entry, enlightenment, when it begins to unfold, is so simple. Spirit/God does not make it difficult; we do. It has to do with getting to the place where we want to be—present to God. We think it has to do with meditating so many minutes a day or changing how we talk or looking holy. It doesn't. Those things may jostle our consciousness, but they don't necessarily bring us enlightenment.

Enlightenment *is* simply knowing beyond doubt that Spirit/God is, that Spirit/God Love is absolute and unconditional and that our connection with every living thing is that Love. Once I realized that, I didn't have to look for or see the spirit in everyone else, because I *know* that this Love is what I share with everything and everyone.

Among the many messages that Mary has shared with the Medjugorje visionaries, one emerges as most clear and relevant to me: Peace begins in the heart of the individual. The Blessed Mother said in 1985, "Dear children: Everything has its time. Today, I invite you to start working on your hearts. All the work in the fields is finished. You find time to clean the least important places but you leave your hearts aside. Work more and with love, clean your hearts."

If you dream of peace on Earth, do not say it is impossible until you have made peace within yourself. It is not difficult; we are advised to pray and fast. To decide for peace takes just a little willingness to change our priorities. A physical pilgrimage allows just that—a shift of priorities by changing our environment and changing our focus for a week or so.

The inner pilgrimage is the same—a shift of priorities so that we become one with who we already are.

# 2011 INFORMATION UPDATE

## THE VISIONARIES

*(Information from Medjugorje.org, date updated unknown, accessed August 21, 2011)*

### Ivanka Ivanković-Elez

Ivanka was the first to see Our Lady on June 24, 1981. Born in 1966, she is the youngest female among the visionaries. She lived in Mostar and stayed with her grandmother in Bijakoviçi during the summers to help in the fields. Bijakoviçi is one of the five villages in the Medjugorje parish. Ivanka asked Our Lady about her mother who had died that May and was told she was in heaven. Ivanka has seen and spoken to her mother five times over the years.

Mary has given each visionary a prayer mission; Ivanka's is to pray for families. She had daily apparitions until May 7, 1985, when she received the tenth secret. From that time, she has an apparition on the anniversary of the apparitions. Ivanka lives in Medjugorje with her husband. They have three children.

### Mirjana Dragicevic-Soldo

Mirjana was born in 1965 in Sarajevo and also spent summers with her grandmother in Bijakoviçi. She was walking with Ivanka the day she first saw the apparition.

Her prayer mission from Our Lady is to pray for unbelievers. Her daily apparitions ended December 25, 1982, when she was the first seer to receive the tenth secret. Mary now appears to Mirjana annually on her birthday, March 18. Since August 2, 1987, Our Lady also visits Mirjana on the second day of each month to pray with her for all unbelievers. Mirjana tells us that Our Lady defines "unbelievers" as those who have not yet felt God's love. A graduate of the University of Sarajevo, Mirjana lives in Medjugorje with her husband, Marko Soldo. They have two daughters.

**Marija Pavlović-Lunetti**

Marija was born in 1965 in Bijakoviçi. When the apparitions began, she was studying in Mostar eighteen miles from Medjugorje.

Her prayer mission is to pray for the souls in Purgatory. She still has daily apparitions and is the visionary to whom Our Lady gives a public message to the world on the twenty-fifth of each month. She has been given nine secrets. Marija lives in Italy with her husband and has four children. She visits Medjugorje a number of times each year.

**Vicka Ivanković-Mijatović**

Born in 1964 in Bijakoviçi into a family of eight children, Vicka is the oldest of the visionaries. She is not related to Ivanka although their surnames are the same. Between 1982 and 1984, Mary dictated her life story to Vicka; she will tell Vicka when the time is right for publication.

Vicka's prayer mission is to pray for the sick. She has received only nine of the secrets and still has daily visitations. She and her husband, Mario, have two children and live in the small village of Gradac, a few kilometers north of Medjugorje.

**Ivan Dragicević**

Born in 1965, Ivan is the older of the two male visionaries. Ivan and Mirjana share the same last name and are both from the village of Bijakoviçi, but are not related.

His prayer mission is to pray for priests and the youth of the world. Our Lady offered to show Ivan his future and he accepted. He says, "I'm sorry Our Lady revealed my personal future to me. [But] I'm content now and not afraid, because I know who guided me. Now, I look to the Mother who guides me, and I live in complete contentment." He sees the apparition daily and has received nine secrets.

Ivan married Laureen Murphy, Miss Massachusetts of 1990, after meeting her in Medjugorje, where she experienced a conversion. They have four children and split their time between Medjugorje and Boston.

## Jakov Ĉolov

Jakov was born in 1971 in Bijakoviçi and is the youngest of the six seers. Jakov's mother died in 1983, leaving him to feel orphaned because his father was absent, working in Germany.

His prayer mission is to pray for the sick. Jakov had daily apparitions until September 12, 1998, when he received the tenth secret. He now receives an annual visitation on Christmas Day. Jakov lives with his wife and their three children in Medjugorje.

# THE SECRETS

*(Information from medjugorje.org/overview.htm, last modified March 19, 2011, accessed August 22, 2011)*

Little is known about the secrets of Medjugorje. The only one completely revealed is the third secret: At the conclusion of the apparitions, a permanent sign will be left on Mount Podbrodo at the site of Our Lady's first appearance. We also know that the evil that faced the world that was contained in the seventh secret was eliminated by prayer and fasting. Although the contents of the ninth and tenth secrets are unknown, they are chastisements for the sins of the world and cannot be eliminated as the seventh was, but can be lessened by prayers and fasting.

When Marija, Vicka, and Ivan each receive the tenth secret, they, like Mirjana, Jakov, and Ivanka, will quit receiving visitations daily. After that, Our Lady will give three warnings in the form of events on earth. These events will occur during Mirjana's lifetime. Ten days before each of the warnings, she will advise Father Petar Ljubicić, who will pray and fast with her for seven days. Three days before each event Father Petar will announce to the world what, where, and when the event will occur. According to medjugorje.org, "after the first warning, the other two will follow in a rather short period of time. After the permanent sign appears on Mount Podbrodo there will be little time for conversion. For that reason, the Blessed Virgin invites us to urgent conversion and reconciliation. The permanent sign will lead to many healings and conversions before the secrets become reality. According to Mirjana, the events predicted by the Blessed Virgin are near. By virtue of this experience, Mirjana proclaims to the world: 'Hurry, be converted; open your hearts to God.'"

## THE LEGITIMACY OF THE APPARITIONS

*(Information from Catholic Apologetics www.catholicapologetics.info/catholicteaching/privaterevelation/Medjacon. htm, date updated unknown, date accessed August 22, 2011.)*

The Catholic Church gives two guidelines for judging the legitimacy of apparitions of the Virgin Mary: "alignment of the apparitions with Church doctrine and the approbation of the Church. If either guideline is negated, the apparition is considered false and "therefore from the Devil."

Monsignor Žanić of Mostar, the bishop in the diocese to which Medjugorje belongs, had the initial duty of determining the legitimacy of the Medjugorje apparitions. He formed a diocesan commission to do an impartial inquiry into the events.

"After a few years of thorough and intense investigative study, which the Church always exercises to determine an unmistakable decision in these matters, the Bishop issued a statement in 1986 giving the results of the study. In the statement, Msgr. Žanić condemned the apparitions as not made by the most Holy Virgin Mary and he forbade the pilgrimages set up from the beginning without ecclesiastical approval by the pastor of Mostar."

Bishops on three subsequent commissions or committees reached the same conclusion, the last submitted in 1990.

"A Vatican doctrinal official said the bishops' statement against defining the apparitions as supernatural should be accepted by the faithful around the world.

"Regardless of these testimonies by the most competent authorities in the Church, many refuse to heed the Church's decision and persist in going to Medjugorje. One wonders what authority would be sufficient to convince these travelers of the truth of the Church's clear and emphatic declaration. It is also disturbing to consider that, if the 'apparitions' are not from God, from whence do they originate?"

The Catholic Apologetica paper referred to here compares the teachings of the Church and scripture with the "revelations" of Medjugorje:

| WHAT THE CHURCH SAYS | WHAT MEDJUGORJE SAYS |
|---|---|
| "There is but one universal Church of the faithful outside of which no one at all can be saved." ~ *Pope Innocent III* | "**God presides over all religions as a king controls his subjects, through his priests and ministers.**" ~ Svetozar Krljević O.F.M., *The Apparitions of Our Lady of Medjugorje*, Franciscan Herald Press, 1984. |
| "We declare, say, define, and pronounce that it is absolutely necessary for the salvation of every human creature to be subject to the Roman Pontiff." ~ *Pope Boniface VIII, The Bull Unnam Sanctum 1302 A.D., Ex cathedra.* | "**The Madonna always stresses that there is but one God and that people have enforced unnatural separation. One cannot truly believe, be a true Christian, if he does not respect other religions as well.**" ~ "Seer" Ivanka Ivanković, *The Apparitions of Our Lady of Medjugorje*, Franciscan Herald Press, 1984. |
| "The most Holy Roman Catholic Church firmly believes, professes, and preaches that none of those existing outside the Catholic Church ... can have eternal life." ~ *Pope Eugene IV, The Bull Cantate Domino 1441 A.D., Ex cathedra.* | "**The Madonna said that religions are separated in the earth, but the people of all religions are accepted by her Son.**" ~ "Seer" Ivanka Ivanković, *The Apparitions of Our Lady of Medjugorje*, Franciscan Herald Press, 1984. |
| "That **they may be one**, as thou Father, art in me and I in thee, that they also may be one in us; that (as a consequence) the world may believe that Thou hast sent me." ~ *John 17:21* | |

| WHAT THE CHURCH SAYS | WHAT MEDJUGORJE SAYS |
|---|---|
| "Endeavoring to keep the unity of the Spirit in the bond of peace. There is **one body and one spirit** even as ye are called in one hope of your calling. One Lord, one faith, one baptism." ~ *Ephesians 4:3-5* | Question: "Is the Blessed Mother calling all people to be Catholic?" "No. **The Blessed Mother says all religions are dear to her and her Son.**" ~ "Seer" Vicka Ivanković, Janice T. Connell, *The Visions of the Children, The Apparitions of the Blessed Mother at Medjugorje,* St. Martin's Press, August, 1992.<br><br>**"The Blessed Mother has said: 'Tell everyone that it is you who are divided on earth. The Moslems and the Orthodox for the same reason as Catholics, are equal before my Son and me.'"** |

The article ends by saying that given these comparisons one must either conclude that the doctrines of the Church and scripture are erroneous in their "infallible teachings," or that the Medjugorje apparitions are false.

*Author's Note: The single message that allowed me to embrace Mary and her teachings is that all religions are equal; this is the primary reason the Church repudiates the apparitions.*

CHAPTER TWO

# HONORING THE EXPERIENCE

*We shall not cease from exploration*
*And the end of all our exploring*
*Will be to arrive where we started*
*And know the place for the first time.*
~ T.S. ELIOT

HAT WAS THIS EXPERIENCE I HAD IN MEDJUGORJE? What did it mean? Why me? Why Mary? What was I to do with it? These were a few of the questions that reverberated through my mind as I began to seek some kind of balance in my life upon my return.

I had to pray for balance. I had to pray that the state of bliss would become grounded. For two weeks, I had trouble driving a car because I could not remember how to use the pedals. To live in this world, we need to be grounded. We need our minds as well as our hearts.

I knew very little about Mary, about the history of apparitions, or about how such intense experiences *really* affected people's lives. On the level of the heart, I wanted to be sure I never lost it and on the level of the mind, I wanted to understand it.

Above all, I wanted to keep my experience, to honor it by making it part of my life. I seemed to need, however, some context for it. A verification, not that it had happened, but that it did indeed relate to my way of being in this world and related also to life itself. I had been told to "take this and go out into the world." For me, this meant to share with others what had happened. When I gave my first talk, I was asked if I was worried about speaking. I said from some deep place of knowing it as true, "When you teach from the heart, you do not need to be afraid." This was the beginning of my honoring my own experience.

As I went out into the world, I began to realize that encounters with God are far more common than I had believed. Quite ordinary people have visions, illuminations, or visitations of Holy Beings in dreams. It is probable that these experiences are not extraordinary at all.

Thomas Aquinas said, "Whatever is received is received according to the mode of the receiver."[1] It is not unusual then that Mary, who is considered the Queen of the Apostles and the Mother of the Church and is revered, honored, and cherished by Catholics everywhere, should be a common apparition. It is also not unusual that the form of her messages and directions are always very Catholic. These are the images, words, and form that the recipient understands. As an apparition, Mary is usually of the same race as the seer and often dressed in native clothing. She speaks the seer's language. Usually, she appears to the poor and to children.

Non-Catholics may be more likely to have dreams or visional encounters with Holy Beings like Jesus, Quan Yin, or angels rather than with Mary. Many people, regardless of religious background, experience dreams of profound spiritual content, moments of extreme clarity in which there is a sudden inner knowing of the oneness of the universe, or the experience, with another person, of feeling as though the souls of both people joined outside their bodies.

These special moments arc difficult for people to talk about. They are so personal, so real, and so holy that there is a fear of casting our pearls before swine.[2] The Western, rational, primarily Protestant mind does not accept the intuitive or the "supernatural" with ease. Catholics, however, have visions and apparitions as an integral part of their belief system. Although the Catholic Church does not require belief in apparitions, it does accept their possibility.

When we begin judging our own experience, we can lose its spiritual content. Some people, after having intense spiritual experiences, feel bitter and rejected when the experience is not repeated. I view these experiences as wake-up calls. We can wake up and pay attention or we can go back to sleep. If we go back to sleep, we cannot expect the telephone to keep ringing. Once we are awake, we may not need to be called again. We are responsible for what we do with the experience, for keeping it alive. Where this inner pilgrimage takes us, when we choose to follow, is to the knowledge that each moment is holy. When we touch on this truth, we experience true joy.

Some experiences are called "miracles." This term is usually applied to physical healings or to some manifestation in the physical world that is unprecedented or contrary to "natural law." Remembering that Mary has said that through prayer we can reverse natural law, clearly brings into question whether or not miracles need to be viewed as unusual. To paraphrase Kenneth Wapnick, there is really no difference between curing the hangnail and curing cancer.[3] In either case, the "natural law" is reversed. Miracles can be more broadly viewed as a change in perception, a shift in inner knowing, and a synchronistic event. Miracles happen all the time whether or not we are aware of them. Therefore, the more aware we become, the more frequent the miracles.

In Medjugorje, there have been physical healings as well as inner healings. There is the parchment given to Mirjana that is of an unrecognizable material. Vicka's headaches, which doctors had traced to an inoperable benign cyst on the brain, have been healed. She revealed in September, 1988 that she had agreed with Mary to suffer the headaches in order to release souls in Purgatory. There are also the signs—the miracle of the sun, the spinning of the cross on Cross Hill, writings and visions in the sky. There is to be a permanent sign left on Mount Podbrodo, the Hill of the Apparitions.

Similar miracles have been associated with apparitions in the past. In 1531 at Guadalupe, Mexico, Mary gave the Indian Juan Diego her portrait on his cape to prove her authenticity to his Bishop. This portrait is above the altar in the Church of Our Lady of Guadalupe. The fabric of the cape is unaltered by over four centuries even though for many of these years the cape was unprotected. The paint cannot be associated with any that is known. Since the 1830s, there has been an increase in the number of Marian appearances. Over two hundred visions have been reported; only ten percent have been proved to be fake. All the apparitions have similar signs, miracles, and messages associated with them. At Fatima, Portugal, in 1918, thousands saw the sun spin and approach the earth and recede again to heaven. At Lourdes, France, in 1858, a healing spring sprang from the earth where no spring had been. The bodies of two seers, Bernadette Soubirous of Lourdes and Catherine Labouré, who had an apparition in a Paris convent in 1830, remain uncorrupted.

*I beg you, destroy your house made*
*of cardboard which you have*
*built on desires.*
*Thus I will be able to act for you.*
~ For Jelena's group, 1986

In early Judaeo-Christian history, miracles of this sort abounded. Many Biblical stories are about people who had visitations from angels, dreamed transformative dreams, heard God's voice, or experienced foreknowledge of events. Even people who are very literal in their belief of Biblical stories, however, have difficulty accepting that angels, visions, and other miracles can happen today to ordinary people. We have no difficulty accepting electricity in our homes, although few of us can explain or even conceive of how it works. Radio waves filled the air before radios were present to receive them. At any point in history, people believe that their present science is infallible and that they can explain the workings of the universe. At the same time they laugh at the misconceptions of the science of the past. The true scientist, however, is engaged in journeying into the mystery of the unknown rather than in proving that which is believed to be true is true. In *Hamlet* Shakespeare wrote, "There are more things in heaven and earth, Horatio, than are dreamed of in your philosophy."[4] We, however, remain attached to our philosophy of what is "real."

We are not asked to believe without thinking, but to open our minds to the possibilities. Change will occur whether or not we resist it. Resisting change is like swimming against the current. If we only turn around, we will go where we need to go with very little effort. As I have searched for understanding of my own experience, I realize that I can no longer hide behind the maybe. I can say that I now believe that in God, anything and all things are possible.

We all search for a connection with the Universe and for the meaning of our experience. This is our pilgrimage on this earth. Deep within us lives a desire to be united with one another and with God. We seek Love in its most sublime form. Unfortunately, for some of us the realization of the need for this pilgrimage does not occur until the time of physical death. Some people choose to deny their spiritual sides and to live their lives in darkness rather than in light. Usually out of some pain in their pasts, they seek to control and manipulate their physical realities to achieve success in human terms. It is not until physical illness or death threatens or some other intense personal trauma occurs, that they are willing to admit that they do not have control. Then they may turn to an inner search to make their peace with God.

No matter why or how we embark on our search or how circuitous our journey, the destination is the same. This book and this message is entitled *Mary's Way*, yet I firmly believe it could just as easily be entitled *Jesus' Way* or *Buddha's Way* because the lessons, the curriculum, is the same for all. Once the dogma, the doctrine, and the form are stripped away, there is only one way to God.

The deeper my search for context and understanding has gone, the deeper I have begun to realize that my life is the context. There is no difference between my life, day to day, and my experience before the Blue Madonna in St. James Church. The only limits are the ones I myself impose. The experience I am growing to honor is the total moment-by-moment experience of life itself. I think this is what Mary is teaching. It is simple. It is all about Love.

*If you live the messages you are*
*living the seeds of holiness.*
—October 10, 1985

CHAPTER THREE

# OPENING THE HEART

*I give you my heart, accept it!*
~ OUR LADY, October 29, 1983

TRUE KNOWING CANNOT BE LEARNED THROUGH THE IN-TELLECT. This is the knowing of the heart. It is at this level that all our being is integrated. When the heart is open the mind, the will, the emotions, and the heart come together as a whole.[1]

Father Jozo Zovko, parish priest at the beginning of the Medjugorje apparitions, tells the story of how he and his congregation learned what it means to open the heart. In the beginning, Father Jozo had grave doubts about the authenticity of the apparitions because, he says, "All my fears would not let me believe it." When Mary said, "Please be converted," Father Jozo thought she was calling those who had left the Church, had quit praying, or had abused alcohol or their families. But then she said, "I am calling you, my son. Why are you looking to them?" He understood this to mean that she wanted to awaken those who were close to her, not address those who were lost. This was only part of what he needed to understand about conversion, so Mary said, "Pray!" He shared this with the assembled masses and the next day everyone was praying—in the church, in the fields, in the homes, and in the schoolyard.

Mary was pleased, but she appeared again and said, "When you pray, do not only say the words, do not only pray with your lips, pray with your heart." Father Jozo was not sure what this meant, but he imagined that

29

"this could be done through a deep, simple meditation, through extreme concentration and calmness of our mind, or through some simple activity." He continues, "Obviously I was mistaken. I was also thinking about other things, as to what prayer with the heart might mean. All my thinking did not help much and I did not know what she was asking for, and she knew it." She sent a message that said, "Before you start praying again today, look within your heart to find all your enemies. Forgive one another. Forgive everybody. Recommend them to our Father with joy. Pray for them. Then wish them a great blessing, joy, and great love."

Father Jozo says:

> At first I thought it was not very difficult. I repeated this message in the church, word by word. I asked them whether it was clear what Our Lady wanted. They said they understood. When I asked them whether we were going to do this, the church remained in silence. You can imagine, thousands of people silent in front of me. It was impossible to say yes to Our Lady. They could not lie. Although they met Our Lady every day the people could not say yes. They remained silent.

Father Jozo experienced a great shock at the deep and empty silence. Not knowing what would happen, he said, "Listen to me; now we are going to pray for that gift. Pray in your heart. Close your eyes, go deep down into your hearts and pray to God to grant us the gift to be able to forgive."

> The painful silence started again, the struggle inside ourselves. With fear in my heart I began to suspect: "Oh my God, what can I do for these people? We cannot truly pray, if we cannot forgive. Because we cannot forgive, we cannot truly pray. Our Lady does not let us pray our way because this is no true prayer. We cannot wish everybody well." I prayed fervently.
>
> After twenty minutes of this struggle in the desert, Our

Lady sent us her gift to break the barrier of silence that had been gripping us....As I held all these people in my heart, the greatest sign came.

... in the middle of the church, a man's voice broke our chains, with a prayer from deep within his soul, a prayer that was Our Lady's gift: "Jesus, I forgive them. Please forgive me." Then he began to cry in a powerful voice.

We all cried together with him. Everybody felt in their heart: I must pray these same words. I have to forgive and ask forgiveness of the people and Jesus. And so we all did the same. That afternoon we were all searching for somebody else's hand, as many hands as possible, to squeeze them and say: "Forgive me." We cried, we were happy and we felt we had been forgiven.

For Father Jozo, this has remained the "biggest miracle of so many signs and wonderful moments, among so many changes in people and in nature" that he has experienced in Medjugorje. Afterward, the parish was different because all the envies, jealousies, and petty differences had vanished. People whose families had not spoken in generations began to speak, to share, and to feel for one another.[2]

To say "I forgive" meaningfully, it must be said from the heart because forgiveness is closely akin to compassion. Joseph Campbell defines compassion as "com-passion, shared suffering: experienced participation in the suffering of another person."[3] When we truly forgive another, we share in both his humanity and his divinity. At the level of the heart where true forgiveness occurs there are no differences, no barriers, and no separation between God and man or between or among people. When Mary says "open your hearts," she is inviting us to love and to forgive and is reminding us that there is no love without forgiveness.

How does Mary, the human mother of Jesus, teach us about opening the heart? She was a poor, devout Jewish woman in a time of social and political turmoil. She became a displaced person, a fugitive, and an exile, as well as a mother, wife, and homemaker. Throughout her life, we are told over and over that she dealt with things by "pondering them in her heart."

In the Biblical story of the annunciation, she made a complete gift of self by saying, "Be it unto me according to thy word."[4] This was not a commitment that could be made only with the mind; it had to come from the innermost depths of her being, from her heart. With these words, she became an example of complete surrender and strength by an ordinary person. With these words, Mary risked death by stoning or, at least, social ostracism for having a child before her marriage could, according to Jewish law, be consummated.

*No one of you is a believer*
*until he loves for his brother*
*what he loves for himself.*
"The Moslem: From the Forty-Two
Traditions of An-Nawawl"

Mary's strength and assertiveness are apparent in her *Magnificat*, the speech she uttered after the annunciation when she met with Elizabeth, the mother of John the Baptist. In this speech, she asserts God's intention of liberating the people from a world of duality in which there exist rich versus poor, fed versus hungry, and powerful versus weak. She expresses that loyalty to God requires loyalty to our world and to our fellow humans. She acknowledges the need for community and for communion with one another. Father Jozo explains that "in union with the Church" is the "principle of the original Church, the principle of every Church, throughout every generation....She transforms people and their hearts, so that all could be Church with one big heart that loves with all the people and is for all the people."[5]

Seeking solutions and making commitments by pondering with the heart, rather than thinking with the mind, requires stepping aside and surrendering one's will. We all know that when we make commitments and promises based on our mind's "should" rather than on our heart's "knowing," turmoil of some degree results. Swami Muktananda suggests that we "abandon the pride of doership" by allowing God to accomplish things through us.[6] Father Jozo suggests that we make ourselves humble, obedient, and small because "faith is not what we think it is, but what God sees and thinks it is."[7]

This is and was Mary's approach; this is the way of the heart. We can all learn to say from our hearts, "Be it unto me according to thy word." Mary's messages in Medjugorje have made it clear that we do not have to perform extraordinary acts to reconnect with God. Performing our ordinary acts with love is the true lesson she teaches. Our only function, then, is forgiveness, because this is the only way we can love God and one another from our hearts.

Mary is the real woman who lived her life from her heart. She is also the symbol and archetype of the heart itself, Mother of Divine Love. She invites us to live from our hearts. To learn the peace Mary teaches at Medjugorje, we must heal, integrate, and balance our psyches. If we are to survive, the age of domination of any one sex, race, culture, or religion must end. Some people will have more difficulty accepting this than others. It is an individual acceptance that is needed before there can be a collective willingness.

It is our resistance to what is that creates our pain. Human suffering lies in resisting the call to love God and one another. Within each of us a war is waged as our egos attempt to control and direct the physical world. We learn to defend ourselves by judging others, to preserve our righteousness by making others wrong, and to search for happiness and meaning outside ourselves because inside we fed empty and worthless. We harden our hearts to the Truth of the presence of God in our lives. To open our hearts means we must at least tentatively say, "Do unto me according to Thy will." Even when we doubt our own sincerity, this is the first step of willingness. As we practice our willingness, our psyches begin to heal. Inner peace becomes our only goal and forgiveness our only function.

In her book, *To See Differently*, Susan Trout discusses how by healing our wounds we become available to serve others with similar wounds.[8] Trout calls it "holding the space for someone else's healing."[9] As Mary holds the space for our healing, we can each hold the space for someone else. We are healer and healed, server and served. This is living through the heart.

In June, 1985, Mary told Jelena:

> ... man's heart is like this splendid pearl. When he belongs completely to the Lord, he shines even in the darkness. But when he is divided, a little to Satan, a little to sin, a little to everything, he fades and is no longer worth anything.

CHAPTER FOUR

# PEACE IS A WOMAN, MOTHER TO THE WORLD

*I am the Queen of Peace.*
--OUR LADY, AUGUST 6, 1981

## MARY, THE MESSENGER

MARY HISTORICALLY IS INTERCESSOR AND MEDIATOR BETWEEN EARTH AND HEAVEN, BETWEEN HUMAN AND GOD. She comes to Medjugorje as the Queen of Peace. She says:

I have come to tell the world that God is truth; He exists. True happiness and the fullness of life are in Him. I have come here as Queen of Peace to tell the world that peace is necessary for the salvation of the world. In God, one finds true joy from which true peace is derived.

Her call for peace, then, is more than a call for the absence of conflict. Her peace is a deep inner peace that creates a desire for reconciliation within the individual, the community, and with God. The messages of Medjugorje teach us how to achieve this peace.

The most frequently given messages concern prayer. Related to this, she speaks of love, fasting, and conversion.

# PRAYER

Mary's request to the Medjugorje prayer group is that they spend at least three hours in prayer daily with a half hour in the morning and a half hour in the evening. Throughout the day, they should pause for prayer whenever possible. She says further:

> Pray with great meditation. Do not look at your watch all the time, but allow yourself to be led by the grace of God. Do not concern yourself too much with the things of this world, but entrust all that in prayer to Our Heavenly Father....Avoid television...excessive sports, the unreasonable enjoyment of food and drink, alcohol, tobacco....Definitely eliminate all anguish. Whoever abandons himself to God does not have room in his heart for anguish.

She speaks of having "an encounter with God in prayer," a "meeting with God, the Creator." "God gives Himself to you," she says, "but He wants you to answer in your own freedom to His invitation." She leads us toward prayer without ceasing and suggests that our "life be prayer," our "work offered as a prayer," that everything we do and everyone we meet be an "encounter with God."

The form of our prayer is not important; what is important is our willingness to communicate with God from the heart. Love is based on relationship whether it is human love or Divine Love. Relationship is based on communication. Prayer is a statement of our willingness and a manifestation of our surrender. As Father Jozo's experience tells us, we also cannot truly pray unless we forgive. This is how we can manage to pray without anguish; forgiveness and surrender remove all anguish. We begin by asking, like the Medjugorje congregation, to be shown how to forgive, to surrender and to pray. For those who practice meditation with a mantra, the goal is to have the mantra become a part of the subconscious so it is always "saying" even while one is engaged in other things. This is to pray without ceasing.

The Biblical story of the wedding of Cana provides the key to prayer.[1] In this story, Mary determined that the wedding guests needed more wine. She presented the problem to Jesus, trusting him to solve the problem as he saw best. She told the servants, "Whatsoever he saith unto you, do *it*."

When we pray we define the need; present the problem without presupposing the solution; trust in the solution; and do whatever we are told. Larry Dossey has reviewed recent scientific studies on prayer that indicate most significantly that prayer is effective and that the most effective prayer is one that states, "Thy Will be done." Prayer is particularly effective in situations where the person or event being prayed for is ill, weak, or has somehow strayed from its normal wholeness. The effect of prayer is to return people and events to their natural state, in alignment with their best purpose.[2]

Prayers, besides presenting need, are to reflect our gratitude, our willingness, and our desire for Oneness. In addition, Mary says that "in every prayer you must listen to the voice of God. Without prayer one cannot live. Prayer is life."

## FASTING

As prayer purifies the heart and mind, fasting purifies the heart and body. Although fasting has become almost lost from the Christian tradition, it is an important part of spiritual practice in Eastern traditions.

Prayer and fasting together integrate our heart, mind, and body. Fasting is a way to discipline the mind and body in order to keep God in our consciousness. Mary advises that we fast with the heart. She says, "Charity cannot replace fasting. Those who are not able to fast can sometimes replace it with prayer, charity, and confession; but everyone, except the sick, must fast." Father Slavko Barbarić writes that "fasting with the heart means following the invitation to fast in confidence and trust, even if we find it hard to fast." Through fasting we will find ourselves "growing closer towards God and others," "loving and accepting our own way with God and with Mary," "loving freedom more than slavery to material things" and "deepening our joy in the Lord."[3]

Practically speaking, fasting goes beyond the realm of food and into our actions and thoughts. Mary specifically recommends fasting on bread and water on Wednesdays and Fridays. She also recommends fasting from television and other addictive behaviors and substances. Whatever the fast, it must be from the heart and not from feelings of self-righteousness.

The result of fasting is a change of perspective. We learn about our priorities and see more deeply and differently into the Truth. Father Slavko explains, "Slowly and surely we realize more and more that we are not self-sufficient, and we realize that the whole world cannot satisfy the deepest needs of our human heart."[4] Through fasting we become aware of our attachments. At first, the awareness is confined to that which we are fasting from: food, tobacco, alcohol. As we continue, however, we become aware of other attachments: our material goods, anger, relationships. Fasting allows us to realize that these are mere distractions; they are not what we truly desire and need. Fasting makes us more open to our true need, the need to be at one with God. Father Slavko says, "We need fasting to be able to grow in prayer and especially to grow in prayer of the heart. To say it succinctly, we find it easier to pray when we fast and we fast better when we pray."[5]

# LOVE

Through prayer and fasting, Love comes. Prayer and fasting demonstrate the intention of the heart. In this way we clean our hearts and can open them to ourselves, others, and to God. Most of us have closed our hearts because of pain and fear. Out of fear we react to things that happen and to people around us. We attempt to control our lives by seeking to protect ourselves from further pain. Many of us do not see that everyone is in the same situation; we are all reacting, protecting, closing, fearing—in general, separating ourselves from one another and from God.

The first step of Love is the realization that we are alike in our belief that we are separate from God and from one another. By recognizing that this other person and I share both our humanity and our divinity, I can be forgiving of myself and of him. The next step of Love is to realize that when someone else reacts, rebels, abuses, hates, and so on—it is simply a reflection of fear and pain. It has nothing to do with the object of the reaction. When someone is rude or mean to me, I can choose to see the pain instead of seeing the rudeness or meanness. This is compassion in action. Then I can take the third step of Love, which is to choose to respond lovingly so that I do not perpetuate the cycle of guilt and pain by being rude and mean in return. Responding with love does not mean that I will allow the person to abuse me. Instead I can ask within for the best response, a heart response that preserves my safety and supports my wellbeing.

Mary advises that each day we:

> ... try to conquer some fault. If your fault is to get angry at everything, try each day to get angry less... if you cannot stand those who do not please you, try on a given day to speak with them. If your fault is not to be able to stand an arrogant person, you should try to approach that person. If you desire that person to be humble, be humble yourselves. Show that humility is worth more than pride.

She also says, "You yourselves know what you have to do." This, I believe, is very important. We *do* know what we have to do. In order to love, Mary says:

> ... make a decision for love....love your neighbors... love those people from whom the evil is coming to you and so....you will be able to judge the intentions of the heart. In the power of love you can do even those things that seem impossible to you.... Hatred creates division and does not see anybody or anything ....carry unity and peace....act with love in the place where you live. Let love always be your only tool. With love turn everything to good....

It is up to us then, to choose, to see things differently: to realize that our neighbor IS our self. That no matter what a person *does*, what he *wants* is *love*. In this case there is nothing wrong with giving someone what is wanted. This is how we nurture the Christ Consciousness within; as we learn to love, we accept that we are loved. This is true forgiveness. Whereas a common view of forgiveness is a way of saying, "Because I am better than you, I will forgive you," true forgiveness is saying, "Because I *am* you, there is nothing to forgive." We all have within us the capabilities of the evildoer. Although I doubt that I would physically murder someone, I know I have held murder in my heart. Therefore, I hold within me the same murderous capability as the serial killer. At the same time, I am also "full of grace" and know that I am loved by God. When I look upon the face of the serial killer, I know that he shares this grace and this love with me; there is no difference under God. In these realizations lie forgiveness and the experience of Christ Consciousness, Divine Love.

According to a *Caritas of Birmingham* newsletter, a friend of Marija's tells the story of a woman who wanted Marija to join her on a short trip. In an effort to get Marija to come, the woman used the friend and Marija against one another, playing out a role common to children who want to do something but think neither parent will agree. When Marija and her friend discovered the ploy, the friend was angry and told Marija how bad the woman was. Marija replied, "No, that was love," and indicated that because the woman loved Marija, she would go to any lengths to be with her. The woman acted out of her insecurity, her fear that she would not get what she wanted, yet behind the action was love. The friend concludes:

This incident taught me that no matter what bad someone has done or is doing, there resides within him part of God, a soul, and even though he may have defiled his own soul, it's still from God and I have to see God in him because He Is. To speak ill of someone is to speak ill of God no matter what the justification might be.[6]

# CONVERSION

Conversion means transformation; it is a commitment to return to God. Mary indicates that conversion means "to fast with love, to start fasting with prayer." She implies that conversion is a process not an event. She speaks of the "road to conversion" and tells us "today decide anew for God," indicating that conversion is a daily and maybe even a minute-by-minute decision.

Commonly, the word conversion is associated with becoming a member of a certain denomination or faith. Mary, the Mother, represents inclusive love of her progeny. She expresses love toward everyone, regardless of religious affiliation, Mary Craig writes:

> So it was almost shocking to devout Catholics when the Madonna was reported as saying: "You must respect each man's beliefs. No one should despise another for his convictions. God is one and indivisible. It is not God but believers who have caused the dreadful divisions in the world." To Mirjana she pointed out that devout Catholics seemed to go out of their way to avoid contact with Orthodox and Muslims; yet nobody who refused to take other believers seriously was worthy of the name of Christian. By way of underlining this difficult message, the Lady had singled out one of Mirjana's neighbors in Sarajevo, a Muslim woman called Pasha, for special praise. "She is a true believer, a saintly woman. You should try to be more like her."

Conversion then is not about a religious form, it is about spiritual transformation. At the beginning of the apparitions, Mary said, "I want to convert and reconcile everyone." This suggests that as people transform spiritually and return to God, they are reconciled with one another.

Conversion is related to surrender. In Medjugorje, I felt the Love of God. Later I realized that surrender involved truly accepting this Love for myself, loving myself, every human part of myself. Then I would be able to do what I was asked without fear and without expectation. Then I could live *in* God and not *under* God. This, I believe, is conversion.

# MARY, THE PROPHET

Edward Atzert points out that historically, nearly all prophets were "prophets of doom." In each of the apparitions of the past one and a half centuries, Mary has warned of impending catastrophes. Her prophecies have been accurate.

In 1830, she told Catherine Laboure in Paris of the imminent overturn of the throne and of some very specific events to occur in France in forty years. To the seers, Mathieu and Giraud, in La Salette, she foretold of the great famine that would soon sweep Europe. To Estelle Faguette, in 1876, the outbreak of World War I was prophesied. At Fatima in 1917, Mary predicted a great light in the sky that would precede great evil. People all over Europe witnessed the light in 1939 and one month later, Hitler invaded Poland. She added, "The good will be martyred, the Holy Father will have much to suffer and various nations will be annihilated." Also in Fatima, Mary asked for prayers for the conversion of Russia: "If they listen to my requests, Russia will be converted and there will be peace. If not, she will scatter her errors through the world, provoking wars and persecution of the Church."[8] This is interesting in light of the history of Soviet communism, the recent events in the Soviet Bloc countries, and in view of Mary's prophecies in Medjugorje.

In Medjugorje, three particular prophecies made in 1981 and 1982 have gained media attention: "There will be great conflicts (in Poland), but in the end, the just will take over"; "The Russian people will be the people who will glorify God the most. The West has made civilization progress, but without God, as if they were their own creators"; and "The Third World War will not take place."[9]

I remember reading these before I went to Medjugorje in March 1989 and thinking that the fall of communism was being predicted. I did not believe it possible; however, many others and I were proven wrong.

The other Medjugorje prophecies are the Ten Secrets discussed in Chapter 1. Mary's invitation to prayer and fasting is meant to avert evil and war, but most of all to save souls. According to Mirjana, the events predicted by Mary are near. In addition, the Virgin gave Mirjana the following message, in substance:

Excuse me for this, but you must realize that Satan exists. One day he appeared before the throne of God and asked permission to submit the Church to a period of trial. God gave him permission to try the Church for one century. This century is under the power of the Devil, but when the secrets confided to you come to pass, his power will be destroyed. Even now he is beginning to lose his power and has become aggressive. He is destroying marriages, creating division among priests and is responsible for obsessions and murder. You must protect yourselves against these things through fasting and prayer, especially community prayer. Carry blessed objects with you. Put them in your house, and restore the use of holy water.

Mary states that a full-fledged war is about to start between heaven and hell; she invites all people to join with her in God's plan for the "salvation of mankind." "Do not think," she says, "that Jesus is going to manifest Himself again in the manger; friends, He is born again in your hearts."

In a message to the Marian Movement of Priests, Mary said, in part:

*These are the times of the great return.* Yes, after the time of the great suffering, there will be the time of the great rebirth and all will blossom again. Humanity will again be a new garden of life and of beauty and the Church a family enlightened by truth, nourished by grace, consoled by the presence of the Holy Spirit. Jesus will restore his glorious reign. He will dwell with you and you will know the new times, the new era. You will at last see a new earth and new heaven.

The great mercy will come to you as a burning fire of love and will be brought by the Holy Spirit, who is given to you by the Father and the Son, so that the Father may see Himself glorified and the Lord Jesus may feel Himself loved by all his brothers.

The Holy Spirit will come down as fire, but in a manner different from his first coming: it will be a fire which will burn and transform everything, which will sanctify and renew the earth

43

from its foundations. It will open hearts to a new reality of life and lead all souls to a fullness of holiness and of grace. You will know a love that is so great and a sanctity that is so perfect that it will be such as you had never known before. It is in this that the Spirit will be glorified: in bringing everyone to the greatest love for the Father and for the Son.[10]

Mary has given the visionaries a terrible vision of Hell. She says, "Men who go to Hell no longer want to receive any benefit from God. They do not repent nor do they cease to revolt and to blaspheme. They make up their mind to live in Hell and do not contemplate leaving it." Hell is a choice that we make, as well as experience while on earth. "They rage against God and they suffer, but still they refuse to call on God. They have already become part of Hell while they are still alive." Her description of Purgatory is of different levels, from close to Hell to close to Heaven. People in Purgatory profit from their own prayers as well as from the prayers of those on earth. God permits these souls to "manifest themselves in different ways, close to their relatives on earth, in order to remind men of the existence of Purgatory and to solicit their prayers." Furthermore, "at the moment of death, you are conscious of the separation of the body and soul."

*I wish all your life be love, only love.*
*Everything that you do, do it with*
*love. In every little thing, see Jesus*
*and His example. You also do as*
*Jesus did. He died out of love for you.*
*You also offer all you do with love*
*to God, even the smallest little*
*things of everyday life.*
*~ To Marija while in America,*
November 30, 1988

As humans, we receive prophesy with mixed feelings. If the prophesy is positive, we are ready to believe; if negative, we are ready to reject. If it supports our belief system, we exhort it. If it challenges our belief system, we ignore it. In addition, some of the prophecies and messages are confusing and difficult to comprehend. Father Jozo asks that we "be humble....be open and trust....She is our mother. She is the one who does not criticize or attack. She does not refuse anybody. She addresses us: "Dear children."[11]

Prophecies are meant to warn, not to engender fear. My personal view is that I do not need to understand all that is said or worry about what is predicted; if something challenges a personal belief, I can say, "Well, here is something I don't understand; I will ask for understanding." There is mystery in Creation and within the mystery, wonder. I feel that there are many things beyond the limitations of the human mind. What matters is that I choose to become closer to God because I am discovering that it enriches my daily life and makes any hardships that come my way, easier. Whatever the future holds, I know now that I will do better feeling close to God, than feeling separate. This is true for everyone. D.R. Golob says:

> We all will meet our final hour, our days or moments of darkness, and our trumpet's final call. It may be in a moment; it may be years from now. It will be a private time, a personal journey, for each of us, alone. It does not matter whether one, a hundred, a thousand or a million other souls are traveling at the same moment. Each of us has our own inevitable trip. What matters is that we travel in the love of God.[12]

Mary tells us, "Your responsibility is to accept Divine peace, to live it, and to spread it, not through words, but through your life."

# MOTHER OF THE WORLD

## by Helen Schucman

*Peace is a woman,*
*mother to the world,*
*Whom God has sent to lay*
*a gentle hand*
*Across a thousand children's*
*fevered brows.*
*In its cool certainty there is no fear,*
*And from her breasts there comes*
*a quietness*
*For them to lean aqainst*
*and to be still.*

*She brings a message to their*
*frightened hearts*
*From Him Who sent her.*
*Listen now to her*
*Who is your mother in your Father's Name:*
*"Do not attend the voices*
*of the world.*
*Do not attempt to crucify again*
*My first-born Son,*
*and brother still to you."*

*Heaven is in her eyes,*
*because she looked*
*Upon this Son who was the first.*
*And now*
*She looks to you to find him once again.*
*Do not deny the mother of the World*
*The only thing she ever wants to see,*
*For it is all you ever want to find.*

## CHAPTER FIVE

# LIVING THE MESSAGES

*...what I do in you is up to you.*
—OUR LADY, April 24, 1954

M Y EXPERIENCE AT MEDJUGORJE WAS MY POINT OF SPIRITUAL INTEGRATION. There have been other times in my life when I was aware of making a major shift. I can vividly recall the moment at which I decided that I could choose not to have depression run my life. This was a vivid moment at the beginning of a long process. My week in Medjugorje, however, turned my life inside out immediately and permanently. I should stress that I am very aware that the permanence is by choice. It is not as though I was turned from a frog into a princess by a fairy godmother—I choose and work at staying in princessdom. Sometimes I forget and return to being a frog, but even then, I feel I will never be the frog of my past. Maybe when I forget now, I am more of a frog princess!

In his book, *The Different Drum*, M. Scott Peck defines four stages of spiritual growth.[1] Paraphrased, they are:

**STAGE I. Chaotic, antisocial:** a stage of undeveloped spirituality. In this stage, people's relationships are manipulative and self-serving and the people are basically unprincipled.

**STAGE II. Formal institutional:** a stage of the majority of churchgoers and believers. In this stage, people are attached to the forms of their religion to the point of being fearful of change. Their view of God is usually of an external, transcendent being who, though loving, is also punitive. In their practice of religion, the messenger and the mechanics of the message are emphasized; the substance of the message is often lost. They have little understanding of the immanent, indwelling God.

**STAGE III. Skeptic, individual:** a stage of rejection and rebellion against Stage II. Frequently they are "non-believers"; however, they are often more developed spiritually in an individualistic way. People in this stage are often very active in social causes. They often become seekers who then transition to Stage IV.

**STAGE IV. Mystic, communal:** a stage of acknowledgment of the enormity of the unknown, a love of the exploration of the mystery. With this intense seeking comes an awareness of unity and the awareness that the whole world is a community.

Upon reading Peck's stages, I easily saw that I had been teetering between Stages III and IV, and that Medjugorje pushed me into IV forever. The mystery engages me and the Oneness of all things fills me with joy.

It is interesting to me now, more than a year later, to examine the three requests I made when I went to Medjugorje: to have my heart opened so that I could be more loving, to learn how to pray, and to learn the meaning of surrender. I see now that surrender encompasses everything. Mary demonstrates surrender—the saying yes to God. To do this I must have an open heart. I must pray, I must aim toward giving God my every moment.

My lessons in surrender have been an ongoing process since my return from Medjugorje. Surrender, after all, is dependent on free will. I am finding that there is great fun and joy in learning surrender. Much to my surprise, it is a most empowering and freeing experience.

# SURRENDER

I really had no idea about the meaning of surrender before I went to Medjugorje; the term confused me. I had moved beyond believing that I had to be an ascetic in the sense of giving up all worldly goods and relationships. But I did not know what I was supposed to do. In my mind, I believed surrender was still related to sacrifice and suffering. I had had enough of sacrifice and suffering and did not really want to invite any more guilt and pain into my life.

I see now that Mary's life was one of complete surrender. She was certainly no ascetic in the physical sense. She lived a full, varied, and rich life filled with many challenges. And yet she was totally committed to letting God guide her life. She was a true spiritual ascetic in the sense that she had died to self and been born to Self. She lived her ordinary life in an extraordinary way.

When I returned from Medjugorje there was an acquaintance I will call Kelly in whose physical presence I felt caught in a vortex of incredible and powerful energy. Kelly was interested in my trip, but totally unaware of what I was experiencing. Not only did it happen when we were physically together, but if the name "Kelly" crossed my mind while I was meditating, I would burst into tears. I was so totally disconcerted by what was happening that I could hardly function. I knew this could not continue.

After two weeks of this, I called my friend Susan Trout and asked her help in understanding what was going on. She asked me to describe my feeling of the "energy." I replied that the feeling was what I would feel if my child had been lost and suddenly someone brought him to the door—an intense feeling of love and relief. Susan then asked, "Are you channeling Divine Love?" My answer was an immediate, "Yes!" Perplexed by my own response, I asked, "But why Kelly? What am I supposed to do?" Susan answered, "Remember, you do not have to be the doer."

Following this conversation, I went to a church determined to stay until I had some clarity. I walked into the church and declared out loud, "Okay, God, here I am and I'm staying until I know what this is all about."

I knelt at one altar after another and suddenly "heard" from within, "Tell Kelly...." What followed was a very personal message that had to do with Kelly's childhood. I was stunned because I didn't think it was true. I spent the following two hours arguing with my Inner Voice about the truth of the message, about the fact that I could not possibly say this to someone whom I knew only casually, and about the validity of the Inner Voice itself—how did I know it was "good" and not just my ego or some "bad" voice.

Following more than an hour of "conversation," the Inner Voice suddenly said, "Say ten Hail Mary's." I complied. Then, "Say the prayer you said in Medjugorje." I began, "Mother-Father-God, I come to you in peace and surrender...." The minute I said the word "surrender," I understood. I said the prayer ten times and then the Inner Voice said, "Say the affirmation from *A Course in Miracles*."

*I am here only to be truly helpful.*
*I am here to represent Him Who sent me.*
*I do not have to worry about what to say or what to do*
    *for He Who sent me will direct me.*
*I am content to be wherever He wishes, knowing He goes there*
    *with me.*
*I will be healed as I let Him teach me to heal.*[2]

I knew then that if I were sincere in my desire to learn the meaning of surrender, I had no choice. I said I would do as asked. The Inner Voice said, "It is absolutely safe." And so on a beautiful spring day, a very curious Kelly and I went for a walk and I shared the whole story. To my amazement, the part of the message I doubted was true, and Kelly's acceptance of this process was a gift. As we ventured into a spiritual mentorship together, I once heard the words, "I would sacrifice anything for your salvation. I would cry your tears and endure your pain to achieve your release." At the time I believed these were my feelings toward Kelly since they felt so true. Much later, I, like Father Jozo, was led to ask myself, "Why am I looking at someone else, the message is for me." When the movie *Field of Dreams* was released, Kelly and I laughed together over the similarities. I had been for Kelly a kind of "voice from the corn field" with otherworldly instructions. It was absolutely safe.

The common dictionary definition of surrender is "to yield power to another; to relinquish one's person or possessions upon compulsion or demand." There is another definition, however, which the dictionary designates as obsolete: "to render back; to give in return." It is in this sense, I believe, we are asked to surrender to God. We are to render back to God what we have been given—Love.

We tend to view surrender as "giving away" when really it is "letting go" or "giving up" in the sense of giving upward to God. All that we are asked to "give away" or "give up" is whatever is causing us our pain. The only way to surrender to God is through Love and what is given in Love with an open heart cannot be sacrifice. This is why I believe that Jesus' death was not a sacrifice, not something that should engender guilt in us. He did not die because we are terrible people. He died because He loved us and to demonstrate that death has no meaning and no reality.

God is only Good. We create the fear and the separation as well as the belief that surrender to Good can be anything but wonderful. In the Zen Buddhist book *The Key*, there are the lines, "When you're trying to get what you want out of life, life can be very hard. When you learn to want what you get in your life, life can become very easy."[3] This is surrender. To accept everything that comes in one's life with Love, to give up the belief that we can control anything and to depend on God.

The definition of surrender as "rendering back" is reminiscent of Jesus' direction to "render unto Caesar the things which are Caesar's and unto God the things that are God's."[4] The relationship is reciprocal: giving and receiving are the same on both the physical plane and the spiritual one. And the line between physical and spiritual is getting more and more vague for me. The Presence is everywhere, within and without. My surrender is in recognizing this truth and in practicing it in my life.

# PEACE AND SIMPLICITY

The more I practice surrender, the more I feel a great urging within me for simplicity—to rid myself of distractions. Mary calls us to lead simple lives for many reasons. Our very busy-ness is a distraction—we are caught in a whirl of activities, from exercise classes to television to consumerism. There is nothing intrinsically wrong about these things; however, they can distract us from God. To keep my life simple, I find I must continually examine my priorities. Where do prayer, fasting, and meditation come on the list? When I catch myself drowning in my own distractions, I need to ask, Where is my attachment?" If I am attached to the activity or the object or even the person because I think he/she contributes to my happiness, then I need to examine the attachment and heal my thinking in this regard.

In *The Starseed Transmissions*, Rafael says, "Throughout history, you have been struggling so hard to survive, by your definition of survival, that you have forgotten why you want to survive."[5] In truth, we want to survive to experience true Love. To experience that Love we must rejoin with God. Living in simplicity is a way toward sharing, joining, and communion with others. Simple living is a kind of fasting. The less I have, the less I have to take care of, the less time I have to spend caring for and protecting it, and the more time and energy I have to share with God and with others. In addition, I contribute to the ecology of the earth itself; this illustrates yet again that when I heal myself, everyone and everything, even the earth itself, is healed as well. Discovering simplicity is discovering that I already have everything I need and that I have it abundantly.

# JOINING AND HARMONY

If as a non-musician you looked at the score for a symphony, it would appear to be nothing more than a sequence of chords. When played, each chord has its own harmony, yet alone it is monotonous and unexciting to listen to. By itself, you would not call it music. The true harmony of music is not static or singular; it moves and changes; it flows. In the flow and the change is the beauty of the symphony.

Each of us is a symphony. Each individual is a chorus of members that need to sing together. Life is about getting these parts of ourselves in harmony. We each must learn to know and accept what is within us in order to heal the discordant parts. These parts represent the wounds of old memories or the mimicry of someone else's dysfunctional way of relating. It is here we must first learn forgiveness and healing: here within ourselves. This includes accepting our own dark side.

The easiest way to fine tune ourselves is to watch what we judge in others. What we do not want to see in ourselves, we project on to other people, events, or organizations. Studying our projections tells us how to heal ourselves. As Mary says, "You yourselves know what you need to do." Our answers lie within.

Those around us hear the harmony and disharmony within us through our projections, our way of being in this world. We cannot help but share who we are. This is what Susan Trout calls "our constant state of service."[6]

## WORDS OF THE GREAT SPIRIT

*Look all around you my*
*daughters and sons,*
*at the insects, animals, plants*
*and trees*
*of the forests and fields;*
*at the fishes and the waters;*
*at the birds and the air;*
*and know that they do not need you*
*to survive,*
*rather it is you who need them!*
*Therefore, treat all beings,*
*all things which I have made*
*for MY purpose, gently,*

*with love and compassion;*
*respect them as if they were yourself.*
*Only then can you be free, for truly,*
*you are all MY children.*
~ Billy Micus

Once I was on a train on a rainy day. The train was slowing down to pull into a station. For some reason I became intent on watching the raindrops on the window. Two separate drops, pushed by the wind, merged into one for a moment and then divided again—each carrying with it a part of the other. Simply by that momentary touching, neither was what it had been before. And as each one went on to touch other raindrops, it shared not only itself, but also what it had gleaned from the other. I saw this metaphor many years ago and it is one of my most vivid memories. I realized then that we never touch people so lightly that we do not leave a trace. Our state of being matters to those around us, so we need to become conscious of what we unintentionally share so we can learn to share with intention.[7]

As Mary teaches, to bring harmony to the world, we must create harmony within ourselves. Just as we are each a symphony, we are each a chord in the larger symphony of our world. Mary's saying that there are no divisions under God is of extreme importance. It tells us that there is no duality in God. *A Course in Miracles* states that "the opposite of love is fear, but what is all-encompassing can have no opposite."[8] To me, this means that only God exists. As a result, I will either love and serve God or I won't. There is no halfway. When I choose to love and serve God, then I serve everything harmoniously. This is not a one-time choice; this is conversion in the largest sense. I choose each moment. Sometimes I forget. Then I choose again. I become the larger symphony, my life becomes the dance.

Life is like an infinite patchwork quilt, made up of muslin and calico, as well as satin and velvet, odd-shaped pieces, embroidered together with a complexity of stitches worked in twine and silk. It is rich in pattern, unique in design, and ever unfolding. In themselves, the pieces are nothing but scraps. Together, its beauty lies in its variety and in its unfoldment.

We are not asked to become a homogeneous group of saints with no individuality. Both Jesus and Mary had personalities. We are asked to have honor and reverence for our differences and to see the beauty in the quilt and hear it in the symphony. In this lies peace.

Mary, as I have grown to know her on deeper and deeper levels, is the embodiment of nurturing, guiding, and sustaining Mother Love. Her message is so simple—not easy, but simple.

> Clean your hearts. Forgive. The spiritual symphony begins within.
>
> Live Love, for yourself, your neighbor, for everything and everyone. Love God.
>
> Practice your devotion through prayer, fasting, conversion, and service.

Spiritual growth is a process, not a destination. Few people actually "arrive." This is why Mary asks us to pray and to meditate and to fast—so that we can keep on course, keep our priorities straight. Then our lives become the continual prayer of St. Francis of Assisi.

> *Lord, make me an instrument of Thy peace.*
> *Where there is hatred, let me sow love;*
> *Where there is injury, pardon;*
> *Where there is discord, union;*
> *Where there is doubt, faith;*
> *Where there is despair, hope;*
> *Where there is darkness, light;*
> *Where there is sadness, joy.*
> *Grant that we may not so much seek to be consoled as to console;*
> *To be understood as to understand;*
> *To be loved as to love;*
> *For it is in giving that we receive,*
> *It is in pardoning that we are pardoned,*
> *And it is in dying [to self] that we are born to Eternal Life.*

I have added the words "to self" to this prayer, in keeping with what I believe to be the philosophy of St. Francis: the teaching of forgetting the self in order to remain conscious of Christ within. "Dying to self" does not mean that we must rid ourselves of our egos, our humanity. We need our egos while we are on this earth. At the same time, when we allow this part of our selves to control our lives, we live in pain and suffering because we live separate from God and one another.

"Dying to self" means to realize that there is no separation between one's self and God. As we learn that we are not and never have been separated from God, we die to self and are reborn to Self, our natural state as children of God. As we claim this state of grace, we also claim our connection with all God's creation. As we love God, we love one another and all things. The question for each of us is: Why would I choose to do anything else?

*Every second of prayer is like a drop*
*of dew in the morning which*
*refreshes full each flower, each blade*
*of grass and the earth. In the same*
*way prayer refreshes man.*
*When man is tired, he gets rest.*
*When he is troubled, he finds peace*
*again. Man renews himself and*
*can, once again, listen to the*
*words of God.*

*How the scenery is beautiful when*
*we look at nature in the morning in*
*all its freshness! But more beautiful,*
*much more, is it when we look at a*

*man who brings to others peace,*
*love, and happiness.*
*Children, if you could know what*
*prayer brings to human beings!*
*Especially personal prayer.*
*Man can thus become a really fresh*
*flower for God. You see how drops*
*of dew stay long on flowers until*
*the first rays of sun come.*

*Nature, in this way, is renewed and*
*refreshed. For the beauty of nature,*
*a daily renewal and refreshment is*
*necessary. Prayer refreshes man in*
*the same way, to renew him and*
*give him strength. Temptations,*
*which come on him again and*
*again, make him weak and man*
*needs to get from prayer always*
*a new power for love and freshness.*
*This is why you should pray and*
*rejoice for the freshness God gives you.*
~ Prayer group message,
January 27, 1986

CHAPTER SIX

# EPILOGUE

*Dear children, pray, so that in the whole world*
*may come the Kingdom of Love.*
*How mankind would be happy if love reigned!*
~ OUR LADY, March 25,1986

M Y SECOND NIGHT IN MEDJUGORJE, while I was still believing that I would be the only pilgrim not to have a significant experience, I asked for a dream. I have often incubated
dreams as a way of gaining insight on a problem or issue. This
particular night, I asked, "What is the meaning of Medjugorje for me?"

The dream I had was very vivid in color, detail, and depth of feeling.
I share it here, along with my interpretation of it, because I believe that it
symbolizes the struggle of all humankind.

## THE DREAM

A slightly older girl has attempted to seduce my son. On an impulse he
kills her, then chops up the body and hides it around the house. I, his
mother, am not certain he has done this, but I strongly suspect it. I feel
deep distress because I understand what is happening and cannot help
him if he does not come to me. I do not want to ask him. I want him to
confess to me himself. Even when I see physical evidence in my sewing
basket, I do not ask. I ache with longing for him to come to me. Finally I
suggest that I know.

He confesses, saying, "Why didn't anyone tell me how painful this would be? It is easy to kill physically, but it is so painful afterwards. Why didn't someone tell me!"

I feel this intense, incredible love toward him and say, "Why didn't you tell me? Don't you know how much I love you?"

He responds, "I was afraid."

"I love you beyond conditions," I respond. "Didn't you know that? You must pay the consequences of your acts, yes. And I will always love you." I go to call and realize that I am calling for psychiatric help for him; I am not calling the police.

# THE INTERPRETATION

The ego or human self as represented by my son kills its feminine, spiritual self on an impulse, without thinking. Then he realizes that by doing so he has brought intense pain upon himself. He is afraid to confess his choice, his error, to his mother, the God figure. Then God assures him that he is unconditionally loved and that he must pay the consequences for his actions. The consequences come in the form of his own pain and suffering. God's wish is to assist him in healing his mind rather than in subjecting him to punishment.

This dream, intense and brief, is symbolic of the human condition. We all kill our spiritual selves without thinking and then wonder why we lead lives of suffering and pain. We spend much of our lives denying and avoiding what we have done. Throughout it all we are surrounded by God's unconditional love. We have only to willingly go to Him/Her and confess our desire to see and live things differently. Then She/He will assist us in healing our minds and taking responsibility for our lives.

In the history of humankind, whenever great spiritual truths are revealed, it has been man's role to reshape them to fit into an existing belief system or religious structure. This may well happen to the events of Medjugorje. The universality of the message may be lost in the attempt to contain and validate the event. Rather than remaining as a universal mystical experience, it is possible that Medjugorje will become formalized and institutionalized.

The collective human ego (which some may think of as Satan) may again kill its spiritual self in an attempt to understand with the mind what is gloriously beyond understanding except with the heart. We already have what we seek—the gift of Divine Love. Can we accept it or will we reject it once again? Our Mother is calling us to follow her Way, the way of Christ Consciousness. Each individual must answer the call; not answering is an answer itself.

I pray: Do what she asks without fear.

*Without love*
*you will achieve nothing.*
~ December 13, 1984

*Dear Children, today I am calling*
*you to the way of holiness.*
*Pray that you may comprehend the*
*beauty and the greatness of this*
*way, where God reveals Himself to*
*you in a special way. Pray that you*
*may be open to everything that*
*God does through you so that in*
*your life you may be enabled to give*
*thanks to God and to rejoice*
*over everything that He does*
*through each individual.*
*I give you my blessing.*
~ To Marija while in America, January 25, 1989

# NOTES

Unless otherwise noted, all quotations of Mary's messages are reprinted with permission from *Words from Heaven*, a book of Our Lady's messages from Medjugorje, published by St. James Publishing, P.O. Box 380244, Birmingham, AL 35238-0244.

The 8th edition (September 2000) is published by *Caritas of Birmingham.*

## CHAPTER 1

1. There have been numerous accounts of the events in Medjugorje. For this article, I used two:
   Craig, Mary. *Spark from Heaven: The Mystery of the Madonna of Medjugorje* (Notre Dame, IN: Ave Maria Press, 1988. Originally published by Hodder and Stroughton, Sevenoaks, Kent, England, n.d.) and Hancock, Marie. *Be a Light: Miracles at Medjugorje* (Norfolk, VA: The Donning Company, 1988).
   Quotations of Mary's messages in this chapter were taken from the above sources and from Golob, D. R. *Live the Messages* (Harahan, LA: self-published, 1987).
2. Dragicević, Mirjana. Talk to Italian pilgrims, June 25, 1985. Reported in Craig, *op. cit.*, p. 165.
3. Janz, Denis. "Medjugorje's Miracles: Faith and Profit." *Christian Century* (August 25, 1987), pp. 724-725.
4. Zovko, Fr. Jozo. BBC Interview, Sept. 1986. Reported in Craig, *op. cit.*, p. 162-163.
5. _____. Interviews with Kralijević, Fra Svetozar. n.d. Reported in Craig, *op. cit.*, p. 58.

## CHAPTER 2

1. Aquinas, Thomas. *Summa Theologiae.*
2. *Holy Bible*, Matt. 7:6.

3. Wapnick, Kenneth. *The Simplicity of Salvation*. Audiotapes of a workshop at Ardsley, NY, 7-8 April, 1984. (Crompond, NY: Foundation for *A Course in Miracles*).

4. Shakespeare, William. "Hamlet," Act II, Sc. 5. *The Complete Works of William Shakespeare* (New York: Walter J. Black, Inc., n.d.).

## CHAPTER 3

1. Rockefeller, Steven with Bill Moyers, *Bill Moyer's World of Ideas*, a production of Public Affairs Television, Inc., New York, Show #211, April 15, 1990.

2. Zovko, Fr. Jozo. *A Man Named Father Jozo*. Milford, OH: The Riehle Foundation, 1989 (Includes text of the Nov. 1987 interview that became the video, "A Call to Holiness" prod. by Marian Video Productions of Lima, PA, in conjunction with Medjugorje Witness, Inc. of Bloomington, IN, released in 1989), pp. 24-28.

3. Campbell, Joseph with Bill Moyers, *The Power of Myth* (New York: Doubleday, 1988), p. 174.

4. *Holy Bible*, Luke 1:38.

5. Zovko, *op. cit.*, p. 31.

6. Muktananda, Swami. *Reflection of the Self* (South Fallsburg, NY: SYDA Foundation, 1980), p. 26.

7. Zovko, *op.cit.*, pp. 30-31.

8. Trout, Susan. *To See Differently* (Washington, DC: Three Roses Press, 1990), pp. 55-56.

9. Personal conversation with author, 1989.

## CHAPTER 4

1. *Holy Bible*, John 2: 1-11.

2. Dossey, Larry, M.D. "Power of Prayer: Old Approach, New Wonders." *New Realities*, May-June, 1990, pp. 28-34. Excerpted from Larry Dossey, M.D. *Recovering the Soul: A Scientific and Spiritual Search* (New York: Bantam Books, 1989).

3. Barbaric, Fr. Slavko, O.F.M. *Fasting* (Steubenville, OH: Franciscan University Press, 1988), pp. 45-46.

4. *Ibid.*, p. 25.

5. *Ibid.*, p. 26.

6. *The Caritas of Birmingham Newsletter*, March-April 1990, p. 2.

7. Craig, *op. cit.*, p. 81.

8. Atzcrt, Rev. Edward P. "Our Lady, Queen of Prophets", *Soul Magazine*, Nov.-Dec., 1988, pp. 18-19.

9. *The Caritas of Birmingham Newsletter*, November-December 1989, p. 5.

10. *To the Priests, Our Lady/Beloved Sons*, from Message #357 (St. Francis, ME: Marian Movement of Priests, 1987), pp. 558-560.

11. Zovko, *op. cit.*, p. 33.

12. Golob, *op. cit.*, p. 52.

# CHAPTER 5

1. Peck, Scott. *The Different Drum: Community Making and Peace* (New York: Simon & Schuster, 1987), pp. 188-206.

2. *A Course in Miracles* (Tiburon, CA: Foundation for Inner Peace, 1976), Text, p. 24.

3. *The Key: And the Name of the Key is Willingness* (Mountain View, CA: A Center for the Practice of Zen Buddhist Meditation, 1984), p. 16.

4. *Holy Bible*, Matt. 22:21.

5. Rafael, *The Starseed Transmissions: An Extraterrestrial Report*, The Starseed Series: V. I. (Copyright by K. X. Carey, Kansas City, MO: Uni*Sun, 1982), p. 79.

6. Trout, *op.cit.*, p. 54.

7. Millin, Peggy. First printed in Trout, *loco cit.*

8. *A Course in Miracles*, *op. cit.*, Introduction, n.p.

*Live peace in your heart and in
your surroundings, so that all
recognize peace, which does not
come from you, but from God.*
~ Christmas Day, 1988

# BIBLIOGRAPHY

Atzert, Rev. Edward P. "Our Lady, Queen of Prophets," *Soul Magazine*, Nov.- Dec., 1988.

Aquinas, Thomas. *Summa Theologiae*, n.d.

Barbarić, Fr. Slavko, O.F.M. *Fasting*, Steubenville, OH: Franciscan University Press, 1988.

Boff, Leonardo, O.F.M. *The Maternal Face of God: The Feminine and its Religious Expressions*. San Francisco: Harper and Row, 1979. Originally published in Portuguese as *O rostro materno de Deus: Ensaio interdiciplinar sobre o feminine e suas formas religiosas*. Petrópolis, Brazil: Editora Vozes Limitada, 1979.

Bolen, Jean Shinoda. *Goddesses in Everywoman, A New Psychology of Women*. San Francisco: Harper & Row, 1984.

Campbell, Joseph with Bill Moyers, *The Power of Myth*. New York: Doubleday, 1988.

*Caritas of Birmingham*. Newsletters. Birmingham, AL: Oct. 1989 through June 1990.

Compton, Madonna. "A Plea for Peace?: Modern Miracles of the Numinous Feminine", *Magical Blend*, Issue 28, through Oct. 1990, pp. 67-70, 100.

*A Course in Miracles*. Tiburon, CA: Foundation for Inner Peace, 1976.

Craig, Mary. *Spark from Heaven: The Mystery of the Madonna of Medjugorje*. Notre Dame, IN: Ave Maria Press, 1988. Originally published by Hodder and Stroughton, Limited, Sevenoaks, Kent, England, n.d.

Dossey, Larry, M.D. "Power of Prayer: Old Approach, New Wonders." *New Realities*, May- June, 1990, pp. 28-34. Excerpted from Larry Dossey, M.D., *Recovering the Soul: A Scientific and Spiritual Search*. New York: Bantam Books, a division of Bantam, Doubleday, Dell Publishing Group, Inc., 1989.

Eliot, T.S. "Little Gidding," *Four Quartets*, V, 1942.

Evdokimov, Paul. *La mujer y la salvación del mundo*. Barcelona: Ariel, 1970. Originally published as *La femme et le salut du monde*. Paris: Descleé de Brouwer, 1983.

Golob, D.R. *Live the Messages*. Harahan, LA: Self-published, 1988.

Hancock, Ann Marie. *Be a Light: Miracles at Medjugorje*. Norfolk, VA: The Donning Co., 1988.

Janz, Denis, "Medjugorje's Miracles: Faith and Profit," *Christian Century*, August 25, 1987.

*The Key and the Name of the Key is Willingness*. Mountain View, CA: Center for the Practice of Zen Buddhist Meditation, 1984.

Lao Tzu, *Tao Te Ching*, translation not found.

*A Man Named Father Jozo*. Includes text of the Nov., 1987, interview that became the video, "A Call to Holiness" (prod. by Marian Video Productions of Lima, PA, in conjunction with Medjugorje Witness, Inc. of Bloomington, IN, released in 1989). Milford, OH: The Riehle Foundation, 1989.

Micus, Billy, "Words of the Great Spirit," from *Messages through Meditation*, from a poster in celebration of Earth Day, April 19, 1990, Visionary Awareness, Madison, VA: 1987.

Muktananda, Swami. *Reflection of the Self*. So. Fallsberg, NY: SYDA Foundation, 1980.

Peck, M. Scott. *The Different Drum: Community Making and Peace*. New York: Simon and Schuster, Inc., 1987.

Pennington, M. Basil, O.C.S.O. *Mary Today: The Challenging Woman*. Garden City, NY: Doubleday, 1987.

Pervan, Tomislav. *Queen of Peace: Echo of The Eternal Word*. Steubenville, OH: Franciscan University Press, 1986.

Rafael. *The Starseed Transmissions: An Extraterrestrial Report*. The Starseed Series, V.I. Copyright by K.X. Carey. Kansas City, MO: Uni*Sun, 1982.

Rockefeller, Steven with Bill Moyers. *Bill Moyer's World of Ideas*. Show No. 211. New York: Public Affairs Television, April 15, 1990.

Shakespeare, William. "Hamlet". *The Complete Works of William Shakespeare*. New York: Walter J. Black, Inc., n.d.

Shucman, Helen. *The Gifts of God*. Tiburon, CA: Foundation for Inner Peace, 1982.

*To the Priests, Our Lady's Beloved Sons*. St. Francis, ME: Marian Movement of Priests, 1987.

Trout, Susan S. *To See Differently*. Washington, DC.: Three Roses Press, 1990.

Two Friends of Medjugorje. *Words from Heaven: Messages of Our Lady from Medjugorje*. Birmingham, AL: Saint James Publishing, 1990.

Wapnick, Kenneth, *The Simplicity of Salvation*. Audiotapes of a workshop at Ardsley, NY (7-8 April, 1984). Crompond, NY: Foundation for A Course in Miracles.

Weible, Wayne. *Miracle at Medjugorje: A Series of Columns on a Modern-Day Supernatural Religious Event*. Dec. 1985 through May 1986.

Zovko, Fr. Jozo. BBC Interview, Sept. 1986.

# COPYRIGHT ACKNOWLEDGMENTS

*I wish to engrave in every heart*
*the sign of love.*
*If you love all mankind,*
*then there is peace in you.*
*If you are at peace with all men,*
*it is the kingdom of love.*
~ January 18, 1984

CPSIA information can be obtained at www.ICGtesting.com
Printed in the USA
LVOW10s0353070913

351405LV00001B/43/P